T0360434

"Here, Jason Russell has identified and addressed a void in the available material on labor–management conflict resolution in the US and Canada. His views on how the parties' attitudes, perceptions and ideologies have shaped relationships since the second World War provide for fertile ground on which to reflect and debate."

– **William Dwyer**, *Rutgers University*

Management and Labor Conflict

Management and labor have been adversaries in American and Canadian workplaces since the time of colonial settlement. Labor lacked full legal legitimacy in Canada and the United States until the mid-1930s and the passage of laws that granted collective bargaining rights and protection from dismissal due to union activity. The US National Labor Relations Act (Wagner Act) became the model for labor laws in both countries. Organized labor began to decline in the United States in the late 1960s due to a variety of factors including electoral politics, internal social and cultural differences, and economic change. Canadian unions fared better in comparison to their American counterparts, but still engaged in significant struggles.

This analysis focuses on management and labor interaction in the United States and Canada from the 1930s to the turn of the second decade of the twenty-first century. It also includes a short overview of employer and worker interaction from the time of European colonization to the 1920s. The book addresses two overall questions: In what forms did management and labor conflict occur and how was labor–management interaction different between the two countries? It pays particular attention to key events and practices where the United States and Canada diverged when it came to labor–management conflict including labor law, electoral politics, social and economic change, and unionization patterns in the public and private sectors.

This book shows that there were key points of convergence and divergence in the past between the United States and Canada that explain current differences in labor–management conflict and interaction in the two countries. It will be of interest to researchers, academics, and students in the fields of management and labor history, employment and labor relations, and industrial relations.

Jason Russell is a professor of History and Labor Studies at SUNY Empire State College, USA. He is the author of *Our Union: UAW/CAW Local 27 from 1950 to 1990*; *Making Managers in Canada, 1945–1995 Companies, Community Colleges, and Universities*; *Leading Progress: The Professional Institute of the Public Service of Canada 1920–2020*; and *Canada, a Working History*.

Routledge Focus on Business and Management

The fields of business and management have grown exponentially as areas of research and education. This growth presents challenges for readers trying to keep up with the latest important insights. *Routledge Focus on Business and Management* presents small books on big topics and how they intersect with the world of business research.

Individually, each title in the series provides coverage of a key academic topic, whilst collectively, the series forms a comprehensive collection across the business disciplines.

The Innovative Management Education Ecosystem
Reskilling and Upskilling the Future Workforce
Jordi Diaz, Daphne Halkias and Paul W. Thurman

Management and Labor Conflict
An Introduction to the US and Canadian History
Jason Russell

Creativity, Innovation and the Fourth Industrial Revolution
The da Vinci Strategy
Jon-Arild Johannessen

Performance Measurement in Non-Profit Organizations
The Road to Integrated Reporting
Patrizia Gazzola and Stefano Amelio

Risk Management Maturity
A Multidimensional Model
Sylwia Bąk and Piotr Jedynak

For more information about this series, please visit: www.routledge.com/Routledge-Focus-on-Business-and-Management/book-series/FBM

Management and Labor Conflict

An Introduction to the US and Canadian History

Jason Russell

Routledge
Taylor & Francis Group

NEW YORK AND LONDON

First published 2023
by Routledge
605 Third Avenue, New York, NY 10158

and by Routledge
4 Park Square, Milton Park, Abingdon, Oxon, OX14 4RN

Routledge is an imprint of the Taylor & Francis Group, an informa business

© 2023 Taylor & Francis

Library of Congress Cataloging-in-Publication Data
Names: Russell, Jason, 1968– author.
Title: Management and labor conflict : an introduction to the US and Canadian history / Jason Russell.
Description: New York, NY : Routledge, 2023. |
Includes bibliographical references and index.
Identifiers: LCCN 2022029202 | ISBN 9780367271251 (hardback) |
ISBN 9781032391281 (paperback) | ISBN 9780429294938 (ebook)
Subjects: LCSH: Labor unions–United States. | Labor unions–Canada. |
Industrial relations–United States. | Industrial relations–Canada.
Classification: LCC HD6508 .R87 2023 | DDC 331.880973–dc23/eng/20220711
LC record available at https://lccn.loc.gov/2022029202

ISBN: 9780367271251 (hbk)
ISBN: 9781032391281 (pbk)
ISBN: 9780429294938 (ebk)

DOI: 10.4324/9780429294938

Typeset in Times New Roman
by Newgen Publishing UK

Contents

Acknowledgments

This book has been in progress for several years. It has been delayed by other projects, a pandemic, and a variety of personal and professional obligations. There are past and current Routledge staff whose support I want to recognize including Mary Del Plato, Naomi Round-Cahalin, and Jessica Rech. I particularly thank Brianna Ascher for her patience while work on this book progressed. This is my second book with Routledge; my first one was published in 2018. I hope that I am able to write additional Routledge Focus books that expand on the themes and topics discussed in this one. My father, Thomas Alexander Russell, passed away in 2021 and he was frequently on my mind as I completed this book. He always enthusiastically read my books when they came out, and I am sure he would be eager to read this one as well. This book is for him.

Introduction

Workplaces in the United States and Canada have been shaped by interaction between workers and management, as well as laws, practices, and institutions that largely developed since the 1930s. Laws like the National Labor Relations Act and the Fair Labor Standards Act in the United States, and Industrial Relations Disputes and Investigations Act and various provincial employment standards laws in Canada all began emerging in the pre- and post-World War II years. The arc of the history of work is long and, in the case of work in Canada and the United States, it reaches back to European colonization of the North American continent, which Indigenous people refer to as Turtle Island. Modern ideas of work organization and regulation date back to European arrival as the concept of work that colonists brought with them was entirely foreign to the people already residing in what became Canada and the United States.

This Routledge Focus book is intended to provide a broad introductory overview of key aspects of labor–management conflict in the United States and Canada from the 1930s to the end of the 2000s. It concentrates on relations between unions and management but will also discuss wider influences on interaction between the two groups. It will also provide some background on events and trends before the 1930s and will comment on the state of relations between workers and employers from the 2010s to 2022. The book draws on a range of primary and secondary research sources. Key concepts and readings will be described and referenced to hopefully encourage readers to wade into the vast and rich literature on how relations between labor and management evolved in Canada over the past 90 years. Conflict between workers and employers is usually identified with events like union organizing drives, strikes, and lockouts but it can happen through less overt means. Changes in labor and employment practices in the United States at times had a profound impact on the development of Canadian

DOI: 10.4324/9780429294938-1

workplaces, but there were also important differences between them and key points of divergence that explain management and labor conflict in the two countries.

The first chapter will cover the 1930s and 1940s, which were pivotal years as the labor relations frameworks that exist today in Canada and the United States really originated during that period. The second chapter describes events during the 1950s and 1960s. Those were prosperous decades for unionized workers and corporations, with wage increases meeting or exceeding the cost of living. The third chapter covers the 1970s and 1980s and those decades saw organized labor's power diminish in the private sector in Canada, and in both the public and private sectors in the United States. The fourth chapter discusses the 1990s and 2000s. Those were years when the tumultuous twentieth century drew to a close, free-market capitalism seemed permanently ascendant, Globalization flourished, and workers and their movements felt under constant threat.

Historians have long used that war as a key dividing point when analyzing the twentieth century. The term "post-World War II" will be used in this book, but it has been over seven decades since the war ended and other events and periods will also be described as important in the history of labor–management interaction in Canada and the United States. Beginning this narrative by going back before the 1930s helps frame later analysis. The process of convergence and divergence began early for the United States and Canada when it came to how workers and employers interacted with each other on the job.

The 1800s to the 1920s

The United States and Canada occupy the same continent and seemed to share many social, economic, and cultural traits in the nineteenth century, but they adopted significantly different paths during that period. Thinking about the later development of management and labor interaction in the twentieth century requires discussing the two countries in the years that they were colonized and industrialized. This introduction describes area of convergence and divergence between the two nations and how significant events and trends shaped what came in the century that followed. Both countries experienced transitions from the first wave of industrialization into increasingly developed economies. Workers formed unions, modern management developed, early laws were passed to regulate labor, and governments sided with employers far more frequently than they did with workers.

Working in Colonial North America

The idea of labor–management relations is rooted in European concepts of class and hierarchy. Indigenous peoples in what is now the United States and Canada had social hierarchies, but the idea of deliberately regulating and exploiting another person's labor for profit was unknown in pre-Colonial North America. The problem of how to secure enough workers and regulate work began as soon as Europeans arrived in the Western Hemisphere. Skilled workers had been organized into craft guilds since the Medieval period in Europe, but there were legal restraints on their ability to combine together to regulate their wages. The English law that had the most profound impact on how later labor and employment law would be crafted was introduced in 1351 and was called the Statute of Laborers. That law was passed within the context of major global upheaval caused by the Black Death, which is now otherwise known as the Bubonic Plague. The plague killed between 75 and 200 million people in Europe and Asia between 1346 and 1356. It consequently had a significant impact on work and labor as it reduced the available supply of people to toil in skilled crafts or other work.[1]

Skilled craftsmen in England reasoned that they could demand higher wages since there were fewer of them around to do such things as make furniture, build ships, and erect buildings after the plague. The English monarch responded by passing the Statute of Laborers. It limited how much wages could rise and also compelled men and women to work if they were physically able to do so. This law set an important precedent as it demonstrated that supply and demand did not necessarily regulate how workers would be paid. One of the basic ideas of economics is that the value of something should increase as it becomes scarcer, while its value should become lower as the supply of it becomes more plentiful. The Statute of Laborers showed that the price of labor could be regulated even in times of scarcity.

The Statute of Laborers was followed in 1562 by the Statute of Artificers. That law further regulated wages and agricultural labor, entry to craft occupations, and movement of workers around England. It represented greater control of workers and informed future labor regulation. The introduction of the Statute of Artificers also happened during a period when European colonization of the Western Hemisphere was already underway. Norsemen were the first Europeans to land in North America when they landed at what is now L'Anse aux Meadows in Newfoundland in the tenth century. The Norse, otherwise known as Vikings, did not stay in North America but their fifteenth-century European successors did create permanent colonies.[2]

A large majority of people who came to North America prior to the American Declaration of Independence were either enslaved Africans or indentured Europeans. Slavery meant putting people in bondage, usually for life, but indentured servitude involved a different form of labor. An indentured servant was usually a poor person from Britain, Ireland, or even what is now Germany. Someone who was indentured had the cost of his or her passage across the Atlantic Ocean paid by an agent or potential employer and was then bound to an employer upon arrival in one of the North American colonies.

The use of enslaved labor by Europeans has been the subject of renewed inquiry in the United States and Canada, with the *1619 Project* published in 2019 by the *New York Times* regarded as the catalyst for renewed scrutiny of slavery.[3] American political scientist Adolph Reed, Jr. described slavery as fundamentally being a labor system, and it was entirely about meeting colonial labor demands.[4] Living conditions in what is now the southern United States, below the former Virginia colony and into the Caribbean Sea, were harsh and Europeans succumbed to a range of diseases, especially malaria. European traders noticed that people living in equatorial areas on the west coast of Africa had developed natural resistance to malaria, which was transmitted by mosquitos. The process of capturing, purchasing, and ultimately enslaving people to perform labor in European colonies in North and South America soon followed.

The use of bonded labor would ultimately have a profound impact on all workers across the United States and Canada because it helped shape social hierarchies that were used to classify people regardless of race or ethnicity. The idea that being something other than white equaled inferiority had to be fostered among Europeans in order to justify treatment of non-white people. Playing to such superficial but ultimately compelling distinctions would become part of the labor–management narrative as time progressed in both the United States and Canada. It is also important to note that much attention is paid in the United States to the wording of the Constitution, yet it did not end indentured servitude and more crucially did not end slavery.[5]

Management and Labor in 1800

The terms management and labor were largely unknown in 1800. Workers were divided into two principal groups: masters and servants. The legal framework that governed relations between those two groups favored the first group far more than the second one. Canada in 1800 was still a British colony and would not achieve dominion status until

1867, but the United States had been independent since 1776. Britain's North American colonies were covered by English common law, with the exception of Québec as it retained a legal framework centered on civil law. The United States adopted a written constitution that emphasized property rights, and common law still influenced American jurisprudence.

Organizing a union could be legally considered a criminal conspiracy in the early nineteenth century. British law continued to shape the employment framework in what became Canada after the United States achieved independence in 1789. There was considerable agitation for social reform in Britain following the Napoleonic Wars, and the impact of that agitation reverberated across the Atlantic Ocean. A landmark example of social unrest occurred in 1819 when protestors in Manchester, England demanding political reform were charged by armed troops. The Peterloo Massacre, as the event became known, involved the deaths of 18 people and injuries to another 650 on August 16, 1819.[6]

British workers were also employed within the wider context of the British Empire, and Canadian workers were part of that imperial system. Britain used a mercantilist economic system, which essentially meant the importation of raw materials from its colonial possessions and the manufacture and export of finished goods. Steam power was in its infancy in the early nineteenth century, and the operation of machinery, agriculture, and transportation was accomplished through the use of animal, wind, and waterpower. The legality of organized labor began to change in the 1820s in Britain and in the 1840s in the United States. There were Combinations Acts passed in Britain in 1799 and 1800 that were designed to prevent strikes and collective worker action.[7] The Luddites, a group of labor radicals who derived their names from a possibly fictional figure called General Ned Ludd, engaged in sabotage of machinery in weaving mills in Northern England. The British government responded with The Destruction of Stocking Frames, etc. Act 1812 to criminalize the damaging of manufacturing equipment.[8] The tragic events of Peterloo in 1819, and the public uproar that followed, helped induce the British government to repeal the Combinations Acts in 1824 and 1825. Britain's North American colonies, including what became Canada, felt the influence of events across the Atlantic Ocean.

British unions were no longer illegal, but workers could still be prosecuted for swearing illegal oaths, which was a legally dubious concept. In 1834, a group of six workers in Dorset, England, were indeed convicted of swearing such an oath. They were betrayed by a coworker, charged and convicted, then sentenced to transportation to Van

Diemen's Land which is now known as Tasmania. Australians would later take some pride in the fact that their country was initially settled by convicts, but many of the people sent to the other side of the world were barely guilty of crimes. Such was the case with the six workers from Dorset, who became known as the Tolpuddle Martyrs.[9]

There was considerable criticism of the conviction of the Tolpuddle Martyrs – a massive demonstration was held in London, England by supporters of the six men – and their convictions were overturned and they were returned to England. Several of them, including George Loveless, settled in Upper Canada. There was also a link between the Tolpuddle Martyrs and an important political reform movement in England called Chartism. Chartists wanted the electoral franchise, meaning the right to vote, extended to all male voters in England and George Loveless had some involvement with Chartism.

The conviction of the Tolpuddle Martyrs in 1834 was followed by the 1837 rebellions in Upper and Lower Canada, which would respectively eventually become the Canadian provinces of Ontario and Québec. The 1837 rebels in Canada did not invoke the cause of the Tolpuddle Martyrs when they challenged the ruling establishments of both colonies, but they were agitating for political reform. The rebellions were repressed by force, with many rebels killed in Lower Canada, and the struggles in Canada, in turn, helped inspire Chartists on the other side of the Atlantic. Unions still remained illegal in the Canadian colonies and workers could find themselves in front of magistrates if they went on strike.[10]

The legal status of workers and their unions also changed in the United States during the same years that Chartism was being debated in England and Canadian workers were chafing at a lack of democratic representation in their colonial assemblies. In 1842, the Massachusetts Supreme Judicial Court issued a ruling in the *Commonwealth v. Hunt* case. In 1835, the Boston Journeymen Bootmakers' Society – a craftworkers' organization – demanded that an employer fire one of its members because he would not obey the organization's rules on wages. The employer did so, but a conspiracy charge was brought against the union by the local district attorney. A lower court ruled against the union and issued a conspiracy conviction. Justice Lemuel Shaw heard the case on appeal and ruled that it was not a conspiracy if workers were simply combining together. *Commonwealth v. Hunt* established that unions were legal, although the exact parameters in which they could operate would be in dispute into the third decade of the twentieth century.[11]

The first Trade Union Act was passed in Britain in 1871.[12] The Trades Union Congress had already been founded in 1868. Canada's first Trade Union Act was passed in 1872, largely in response to workers advocating for the introduction of a nine-hour workday.[13] Canadian labor historians have generally not thought about the passage of the 1872 act within the context of what occurred in Britain, but the 1871 British act was surely on the minds of Canadian policymakers when the 1872 law was crafted. Both laws conferred legality on unions but they did not regulate relations between workers and employers.

The terms master and servant began to give way to worker and employer as the nineteenth century passed. There was heightened conflict in American and Canadian workplaces, with similarities and differences between the two countries. The development of the American workplace was different from the experience in Canada for a particular key reason: the centrality of chattel slavery in the United States. There is a common belief in Canada that enslaved labor was not used in Canada. In fact, enslaved Africans lived in Canada prior to the outlawing of slavery in the British Empire in 1833. Indigenous people were also enslaved when France established colonies in the seventeenth century.

Enslaved workers were freed in Canada earlier than they were in the United States but selecting workers for different jobs based on race and ethnicity continued after slavery ended in Canada. Free people of color in Canada still faced widespread social and economic discrimination. The American South, where slavery was most common in the years prior to the US Civil War that started in 1861, was built on stark class distinctions based on wealth. Enslaved workers had no legal rights. Poor white farmers and laborers faced considerable legal sanctions if they challenged their employers.[14]

The years leading up to the turn of the twentieth century saw employers amass greater strength while North American workplaces evolved. The United States experienced its first wave of industrialization in the 1810s, with Massachusetts being the first place to industrialize, while Canada's first wave accelerated by the 1870s. American joint stock corporations developed following the Civil War, and they were important for some key reasons. As described by American historian Alfred Chandler, railroads were the first modern corporations. Joint stock corporations could be widely held because shares in them could be purchased by investors, which meant that people who were entirely separate from running an organization could still own part of it.[15]

Joint stock corporations exerted great influence social, economic, and political influence and it was it was inevitable that they would attract scrutiny from policy makers and academics. Corporate managers were responsible for running an organization but without necessarily having an ownership stake in it. American academics Adolph A. Berle and Gardiner C. Means wrote about the consequences of this change in management and ownership and argued in favor of reforming ownership and management's relationship with firms. They were preceded by a growing chorus of academic critics of corporate power, such as economist Thorstein Veblen.[16]

The first modern unions were organized in the United States and Canada at the same time that similarly new corporations were formed. The Holy and Noble Order of the Knights of Labor (KoL) was founded in Philadelphia in 1869, and its organizational structure and practices were heavily influenced by the many fraternal orders that existed in nineteenth-century America. Its long-serving leader, Terence V. Powderly, was styled Grand Master Workman rather than president much like the head of a fraternal organization. The KoL advocated what would later be called cooperative labor relations and officially eschewed the use of strikes to achieve bargaining objectives. Its members still conducted local strikes in spite of official international union policy. The KoL set an important precedent for North American labor relations as it organized workers in Canada, and thus became an international union. The idea of joining a union based in another country became unusual by international standards but, as later discussion will show, it was common in Canada.[17]

The KoL reached its membership peak in the early 1890s but managed to endure in much-diminished form into the early twentieth century.[18] Internal dissent and the logistical challenge of running an organization that was active across much of the United States and Canada hampered the KoL's success. It was displaced gradually by a far more influential labor organization: the American Federation of Labor (AFL), which was founded in Columbus, Ohio in 1886.[19] It was unlike the KoL as it initially focused on workers in skilled occupations, and generally railed against the negative effect of unskilled labor on the job market. The AFL was additionally comprised of affiliated member unions rather than being one large union that directly organized workers.

Labor became increasingly aligned with the Democrats by the 1920s but that party also maintained extensive ties with the business community. The United States did not develop a viable, national labor or social democratic party. The Democratic and Republican parties, especially the Democrats, housed differing factions that nonetheless managed to unite under common party names. Both parties were ultimately oriented toward free market capitalism, although they adopted differing ideas about how to mitigate its worst effects. Radical politics was often associated with immigrants from undesirable backgrounds, and thus antithetical to American society even though the vast majority of Americans either were immigrants or descended from people who had immigrated from another part of the world. American business supported a two-party political system but did not tolerate the existence of radical parties that espoused anti-capitalist messages.

Canada also had a two-party system from the time of its founding in 1867, with the dominant Conservatives and Liberals having originated in the late colonial period. The 1872 Trade Union Act was passed by the Conservative government in response to workers striking for a nine-hour workday, and Prime Minister John A. MacDonald also saw an opportunity to garner favor with Canada's trade unions. Both the Liberals and Conservatives were aligned with business interests, but nether as thoroughly as their Republican counterparts to the south. The legal framework created by political parties in which Canadians and Americans worked still favored employers, and courts issued landmark rulings that reinforced the power of business over unions. For instance, The United States Supreme Court issued the *Loewe v. Lawlor* ruling in 1908, otherwise known as the Danbury Hatters case, which made unions liable under antitrust laws. The prospect of having to pay damages to employers as a result of antitrust law was an existential threat to unions and, while rank-and-file union members still engaged in work stoppages, their leaders showed less interest in them.[20]

The Canadian and American labor movements were divided into ideologically similar camps in the early twentieth century. Unions in both countries were principally focused on obtaining and maintaining economic gains for their workers, while pursuing social reform. The Industrial Workers of the World (IWW) had an organizing approach that emphasized revolutionary change in the workplace and wider society. The IWW originated in the United States, and its members were commonly called Wobblies. The IWW was active in Canada, particularly in the west, and a short-lived Canadian organization called the One Big Union organized workers and principally operated in the western region of the country.[21]

The decade prior to World War I witnessed the implementation of progressive social and economic policies in response to social inequality and an enormous rise in corporate power. Issues such as working hours, child labor, and health and safety were prominent in the agendas of social reformers. The need for workplace reform was grievously emphasized in 1911 because of the Triangle Shirtwaist fire in New York

City. The Triangle Shirtwaist Company was a firm based in a multi-level building in the Greenwich Village neighborhood in Manhattan, and it principally employed young immigrant women. A fire started on an upper level of the building and quickly trapped workers on the two floors above it. There was no firefighting equipment available or sprinkler systems, and exit doors were locked. The tragic results were that 146 people, almost all of them young women, died either because they were overcome by the immediate effects of the fire or because they leaped to their deaths on the street below to avoid it.[22]

Canada did not have a calamity that captured popular attention like the Triangle Shirtwaist fire, but industrial workplaces were still often highly dangerous, and injuries were common. The first Factory Act, which regulated conditions in industrial workplaces, was introduced in Canada in 1884. Canadian workplaces were dangerous and there were no government compensation plans for people harmed on the job. In fact, the general view was that people assumed implied liability when they entered workplaces and that they were at fault if injured on the job. Employers resisted workplace regulation, while unions advocated for changes to improve workplace safety.[23]

American business often dominated political discourse in the nineteenth and early twentieth centuries, and their commentary on labor was often aggressive and confrontational. The 1892 strike against Carnegie Steel at Homestead, Pennsylvania involved pitched battles between strikers, detectives from the Pinkerton Detective Agency, and the state militia. The latter came equipped with Gating guns.[24] A conflict that occurred in 1914 in Ludlow, Colorado is an infamous example of how labor relations occurred in early twentieth-century America. Workers at the Colorado Fuel and Iron Company went on strike in 1913, and the series of strikes became known as the Colorado Coalfield War. Striking workers and their families fought for better wages and working conditions, and employers were adamantly opposed to giving any economic ground. The National Guard became involved in the conflict when strikers opposed employer efforts to bring replacement workers – commonly called Scabs – into the mines. Conflict reached a climax on April 20, 1914 when armed National Guard troops entered a tent encampment occupied by miners and their families. The strikers fought back as they were also armed, but the guardsmen were reinforced by employer security personnel and the result was 20 dead miners and their families, with children comprising most of the dead.[25]

The Ludlow Massacre became a landmark event in early American labor history. The Rockefeller family, which was known for its ownership of Standard Oil, owned the mine where Ludlow strikers had worked and the family responded to the massacre by implementing the Colorado Industrial Plan. That plan was a form of welfare capitalism, which essentially meant employers trying to cooperate with workers while maintaining unfettered control of a business organization. That plan had a Canadian aspect to it as the Rockefeller family engaged William Lyon Mackenzie King to help craft it. King, a remarkably complex and conflicted personality, wrote a book called *Industry and Humanity* in 1914 and was Canada's first industrial relations expert.[26] He abhorred social strife of any kind and used his book to present ideas on how to resolve workplace disputes. King was instrumental in drafting the Industrial Disputes Investigations Act (IDIA) of 1907 and that federal law included conciliation as a form of dispute resolution. The IDIA promoted industrial voluntarism and did not compel contending parties to resolve disputes. Canada also partially adopted the Whitley Council model, so named for John Henry Whitley, when dealing with federal civil servants in the decades from the end of World War I to the 1960s.[27] That model involved the use of sectoral negotiations between workers and employers, and federal employee associations in Canada unofficially used it when interacting with the government. It would eventually be formalized during World War II. Sectoral bargaining means negotiating labor agreements that will encompass all of the organizations in a specific industry or economic sector.

King was one of a range of people thinking about workplace conflict in the early twentieth century. An approach to industrial relations was built around the work of John R. Commons. Commons taught at the University of Wisconsin and was involved in crafting Wisconsin's 1906 Civil Service Law. He advocated for the use of collective bargaining and against confrontation on the job. His views were not widely shared by American employers in the first decades of the twentieth century.[28]

The pattern of resisting organized labor was prevalent across the United States in the late nineteenth and early twentieth centuries. As Rosemary Feurer and Chad Pearson observed, anti-unionism became a unifying theme for all types of American employers.[29] Much of business opposition to workers' movements was rooted in racism and the enduring legacy of slavery. Business in the northern states wanted the dominant voice of capitalism in post-Civil War America, and it was largely successful as commercial interests in the states of the former Confederacy were predominantly concentrated in agriculture and commodities production. The South, built around a social hierarchy predicated on race, became the most anti-union region of the United States.[30] Heavy industry was concentrated in states like New York, Michigan, Ohio, and Pennsylvania but attitudes about unions and worker dissent were driven by a view that management had to exert absolute control over workplaces. As Sean Wilentz explained in his work on pre-Civil War New York City, employers exerted enormous effort to take control of workplaces and dilute the prerogatives of skilled workers.[31] They were not about to abandon their efforts after their side won the Civil War.

World War I and After

Major national and global crises always usher in significant social and economic change, and World War I fit that pattern. Canada automatically entered the war in August 1914 when the United Kingdom declared war against Germany and its central power allies. The war accelerated Canada's industrialization and the country's entire economy was put on a wartime footing with all areas of production devoted to the conflict in Europe. The early decades of the twentieth century were, as historian Craig Heron has described, the period of the "whip hand" of management. The often harsh nature of management practice has been described by labor historians but less so by business historians. Chandler identified the new levels of management in new business structure structure and focused on the M-form corporation. That form of organization involves dividing a company into departments based on different functions, and having them report to senior management. A diagram of this structure looks like the letter M. The growing size of business functions led to specialization among managers based on the areas in which they worked and the training that they needed for their roles. Whereas business structures had often been owned by one person or family that also executed managerial functions, corporations were larger and more complex.[32]

The early emergence of managerial capitalism accelerated prior to the war years and helped fuel labor–management conflict. This was particularly true of the work of early industrial theorist Frederick Winslow Taylor. Taylor was an American who came from a middle-class family that was disconcerted to learn that he had chosen to apprentice as a machinist rather than attend college and enter a more socially respectable profession. Taylor did not complete his apprenticeship but he did become a foreman at the Midvale Steel Company in 1878. He devised a system of time and motion study that he termed Scientific Management, and his work had enormous consequences on how organizations were managed into the twentieth century and beyond. Taylor broke jobs down into their constituent parts and made managerial control a central part of work processes.[33]

Taylorism informed the emergence and evolution of assembly line production in the United States and other countries. It also gave rise to labor–management conflict in the workplace. Industrialist Henry Ford used assembly production to rationalize and simplify the auto assembly process with both positive and negative results. Assembly line production enabled Ford to exploit economies of scale, which in turn reduced the cost of each automobile that his firm produced. That development in turn helped spur the rise of automobiles as a consumption item and transformed transportation in the United States and eventually Canada. The assembly line additionally robbed workers of their ability to control their own labor as every task was governed by rules meant to maximize efficiency. Taylorism and Fordism were eventually woven to some extent into virtually every workplace in North America. Changes in technology made automation of other work environments much easier, such as administrative tasks. Office work, which had previously been predominantly male, was increasingly done by women as it was automated and unjustifiably considered less skilled.

Taylor and Fordism were followed by, and fused with, the Human Relations School of management. That latter approach to managing people seemed less punitive than Taylorism or Fordism because it advocated using more benign motivation methods. It was associated with George Elton Mayo and was based on studies conducted in the 1920s and early 1930s by Harvard Business School at Western Electric's enormous factory in Hawthorne, Illinois. Mayo was not an industrial psychologist as many people later assumed, and the studies used methodology that was suspect even by the standard of the years in which they were conducted, but they still led to the idea that people were motivated by having attention paid to them and not just by money. This became otherwise known as the Hawthorne Effect. Being nice to the workers and taking a human relations approach to management quickly became a union avoidance strategy among employers.[34]

A combination of different factors including changes in workplace practices, economic distress, employer and government hostility spurred workers to demand social and economic change, and the overall experience of enduring a world war led to widespread management–labor conflict after World War I ended. For Canadians, the Winnipeg General Strike of 1919 came to exemplify the era of labor unrest that followed the war. It is usually portrayed in popular without wider context as a singular incident of labor–management in Canadian history. In fact, the strike was part of a wider pattern of labor unrest across Canada, the United States, and European countries including the United Kingdom.

The 1917 Bolshevik revolution altered the course of World War I as it led to a peace treaty – the Treaty of Brest-Litovsk – being concluded between Germany and the new Soviet Union. The German Army was able to swing enormous military resources to the Western Front in hope of securing a victory against Britain and France. Germany was unsuccessful military, but the success of the Bolsheviks sent a chill through western governments. There were good reasons for the state and capital to fear what happened in Russia. There was a major conflict in Glasgow, Scotland in 1919 between socialists and government authorities.[35] The Boston, Massachusetts police department went on strike in 1919.[36] Major incidents such as those were accompanied by other less publicized struggles.

Labor movements had radicalized since the turn of the twentieth century, and radicals were at the forefront of the struggles that were launched following World War I. The IWW were the leading leftist workers' movement in America during that period, and the IWW applauded the Bolshevik revolution and espoused Marxist ideology. It consequently became a lightning rod for attacks from capital and the state. The IWW was led by competent leaders including Bill Haywood and did not shirk from confronting employers. Workers' movements in the United States and Canada were regrettably divided in the face of corporate power that was generally unified around the objective of maintaining control of economic rewards. Business was still in a position to prevail in the struggle with labor. The business communities in both Canada and the United States had internal differences, but they were unified around the objective of protecting management prerogatives.

Precursor to Two Pivotal Decades

Labor movements in both countries were severely weakened during the 1920s, although that decade was a period of economic, social, and cultural change. The decade became known as the Roaring Twenties – even though economic progress was not as robust as that name suggests – and it came to an abrupt halt in October 1929 with the crash of global stock markets. This event would help initiate a new period of labor–management conflict. The years from 1900 to 1920 gave workers the hope of eventually challenging management on a more equal basis, and of moving from industrial voluntarism to a system that compelled management to actually negotiate with unions.

Management also changed from the turn of the twentieth century to the Great Depression as the M-form corporation described by Chandler became the dominant institution in the private sector. Taylorism was not abandoned and instead fused with the Human Relations School, while both combined with Fordism to later impact aspects of society that were not closely related to workplaces. Labor in the United States and Canada seemed in disarray by the end of the 1920s after suffering major defeats after the end of World War I. The 1930s and 1940s soon brought changes that were unexpected and transformative.

Notes

1 United Kingdom National Archives, "Second Statute of Labourers, 1351", 3 May 2022, https://nationalarchives.gov.uk/pathways/citizenship/citizen_subject/docs/statute_labourers.htm.
2 Oxford Reference, "Statue of Artificers," 3 May 2022, www.oxfordreference.com/view/10.1093/oi/authority.20110803095426927.
3 Nikole Hannah-Jones, et al., eds., *The 1619 Project: A New Origin Story* (New York: One World, 2021).
4 Tom Mackaman, "An Interview with Political Scientist Adolph Reed, Jr. on the New York Times' 1619 Project," *World Socialist Website*, 20 December 2019, www.wsws.org/en/articles/2019/12/20/reed-d20.html.
5 On the history of indentured servitude in the Americas see David W. Galenson, "The Rise and Fall of Indentured Servitude in the Americas: An Economic Analysis," *Journal of Economic History*, 44, no. 1, (1983–4), pp. 1–26.
6 See Jacqueline Riding, *Peterloo: The History of the Manchester Massacre* (London: Head of Zeus, 2018).
7 John V. Orth, "English Combination Acts of the Eighteenth Century," *Law and History Review*, 5, no. 1 (Spring, 1987), 176.
8 The Statutes Project, "1812: 52 George 3 c.16: The Frame-Breaking Act," 4 May 2022, https://statutes.org.uk/site/the-statutes/nineteenth-century/1812-52-geo-3-c-16-the-frame-breaking-act/.
9 Jason Russell, *Canada, A Working History* (Toronto: Dundurn, 2021), 44.
10 On the history of Chartism see Edward Royle, *Chartism*, third edition (London: Routledge, 1996).
11 Patricia Cayo Sexton, *The War on Labor and the Left: Understanding America's Unique Conservatism* (Boulder: Westview Press, 1991), 68.
12 United Kingdom Parliament, Trade Union Act, 1871, International Labor Organization, 4 May 2022, www.ilo.org/dyn/natlex/docs/ELECTRONIC/98373/117044/F1671923749/IRL98373.pdf.
13 Russell, *Canada, A Working History*, 64.
14 See Keri Leigh Merritt, *Masterless Men: Poor Whites and Slavery in the Antebellum South* (Cambridge: Cambridge University Press, 2017).
15 See Alfred Chandler, *The Visible Hand: The Managerial Revolution in American Business* (Cambridge: Belknap, 1977).
16 See Adolf A. Berle and Gardiner C. Means, *The Modern Corporation and Private Property* (New York: Columbia University, 1933).

17 See Robert E. Weir, *Beyond Labor's Veil: The Culture of the Knights of Labor* (University Park: Pennsylvania State University Press, 1996).
18 Weir, *Beyond Labor's Veil*, 321.
19 Howard Zinn, *A People's History of the United States* (New York: Harper-Collins, 1980), 269.
20 Melvyn Dubofsky, *The State and Labor in Modern America* (Chapel Hill: University of North Carolina Press, 1994), 60.
21 Craig Heron and Charles Smith, *The Canadian Labour Movement: A Short History,* third edition (Toronto: Lorimer, 2020), 37–39, 51–52.
22 United States Department of Labor, "The Triangle Shirtwaist Factory Fire," 4 May 2022. www.osha.gov/aboutosha/40-years/trianglefactoryfire.
23 Gregory S. Kealey, *Toronto Workers Respond to Industrial Capitalism, 1867–1892* (Toronto: University of Toronto Press, 1980), 227.
24 Zinn, *A People's History*, 276–277.
25 Ibid., 355.
26 William Lyon Mackenzie King, *Industry and Humanity: A Study in the Principles Underlying Industrial Reconstruction* (Boston: Houghton-Mifflin, 1918).
27 Jason Russell, *Leading Progress: The Professional Institute of the Public Service of Canada, 1920–2020* (Toronto: Between the Lines, 2020), 11.
28 Wisconsin Historical Society, "John R. Commons, 1862–1945: The Spiritual Father of Social Security," 20 May 2022, www.wisconsinhistory.org/Records/Article/CS507.
29 Rosemary Feurer and Chad Pearson, eds., "Introduction: Against Labor" in *Against Labor: How U.S. Employers Organized to Defeat Union Activism* (Urbana: University of Illinois Press, 2017), 5.
30 Raymond Hogler, *The End of American Unions: The Right-to-Work Movement and the Erosion of Collective Bargaining* (Denver: Praeger, 2015), 15.
31 See Sean Wilentz, *Chants Democratic: New York City and the Rise of the American Working Class* (New York: Oxford University Press, 1984).
32 Craig Heron, *Lunch-Bucket Lives: Remaking the Workers' City* (Toronto: Between the Lines, 2015), 229.
33 Harry Braverman, *Labor and Monopoly Capital: The Degradation of Work in the Twentieth Century* (New York: Monthly Review Press, 1974).
34 On Hawthorne and Mayo see Richard Gillespie, *Manufacturing Knowledge: A History of the Hawthorne Experiments* (Cambridge: Cambridge University Press, 1991).
35 Maggie Craig, *When the Clyde Ran Red: A Social History of Red Clydeside* (Edinburgh: Berlinn, 2018), 178.
36 Joseph Slater, "Public Workers: Labor and the Boston Police Strike of 1919," *Labor History*, 38 (1996), pp. 7–27.

1   The 1930s and 1940s

The 1929 crash, which was initially associated with the American stock market on Wall Street, initiated the start of the Great Depression. The economic catastrophe that happened in 1929 and endured essentially until 1939 and the start of World War II was accentuated by a lack of sufficient policy response by government and business, especially the absence of a regulatory framework designed to mitigate the worst effects of the financial crisis. Governments in many instances adopted policies that worsened the global economy in the early 1930s. Most notably, the United States Congress passed the Tariff Act in 1930, known as the Smoot–Hawley Tariff, to raise barriers to imported goods. That act, devised to protect American industry, led to a major drop in American exports and contributed to the rise of fascism in Europe and Japan. Tariff barriers continued to exist between Canada and the United States, although there was relatively easy labor mobility across the border between the two countries.[1]

Massive industrial layoffs began across North America as the full impact of the Depression began to be felt by business. Carefully devised systems of welfare capitalism collapsed as profits fell and corporations went bankrupt. The impact in Canada was initially most acutely felt in the western provinces which were not wealthy and had economies that were heavily based on agricultural production. There were no national or provincial systems of monetary unemployment assistance at that time, and help that was available to unemployed workers was provided by municipal governments. Incomes dropped between 39 and 72 percent across the Canadian provinces between 1929 and 1933. The form of assistance that was available, known as relief, usually took the form of food or other physical items, or low-paid work on municipal projects. The economic impact of the Depression was quickly felt across Canada as industrial workers lost their jobs.[2]

DOI: 10.4324/9780429294938-2

An equally grievous situation unfolded in the United States as farmers and industrial workers across the country began losing their jobs in droves. Statistical measuring techniques in the 1930s were rudimentary by later standards, but it was still estimated that at least a quarter of American workers were unemployed during the Depression years. Up to 15 million Americans – one-fifth to one-third of the workforce – were unemployed by 1933. The actual amount may have been even higher than was officially determined, and industrial production dropped by 50 percent between 1929 and 1933. Conflict between labor, capital, and the state became inevitable in the socio-economic environment of the 1930s.[3]

The problem of labor–management conflict in Canada and the United States in the 1930s was exacerbated by the political orientation of national governments in both countries. Businessperson and engineer Herbert Hoover had been elected in 1928 for a single term, and Richard Bedford Bennett was Canada's prime minister. Bennett was a Conservative and Hoover was a Republican. Their respective parties, especially the Republicans, tended to eschew public policies that would expand the role of government especially if they required new taxes of any type. Income tax was implemented in both countries in World War I as an ostensibly temporary measure that would be discontinued after the conflict ended. The Canadian and American business class was infuriated over the introduction of income taxes, while workers' movements considered taxes on wealthy individuals to be a positive policy change.

Bennett and Hoover were reluctant to introduce policies to alleviate the impact of the Depression, and instead initially preferred to wait for the economic situation to resolve itself. Social unrest, particularly by unemployed workers, led to aggressive responses from governments at all levels in Canada and the United States. The actions of unemployed workers drew the most hostile government response, and two specific events illustrated the hostility that unemployed workers could get from their elected leaders.

The American government agreed in 1924 to pay bonuses to World War I veterans in 1945, but essentially punted the problem of unemployment relief into the future. The United States was only in World War I for one year, but the experience still had a substantial social, economic, and cultural impact on the country. The agreement to pay the bonuses 21 years into the future doubtless seemed like a cheap decision to make for Congressional lawmakers during the prosperous 1920s. The economic disaster of the Depression caused some American veterans to decide that they wanted their bonuses much sooner and a movement began in Portland, Oregon in May 1932 to march to Washington, DC to demand that bonus payment happen immediately rather than in the mid-1940s.

A group of 1,500 men and their families arrived in Washington in June and their numbers gradually grew to between 10,000 and 15,000 as more disaffected unemployed veterans arrived in the capital. Congress was divided over early payment of the bonuses, with the House of Representatives approving the policy change with the Senate opposed. Herbert Hoover said that he would veto a bill to provide early pension payment. He was also worried about the presence of what increasingly looked like a small army of men and their families in Washington.[4]

In late July 1932, Hoover directed General Douglas MacArthur to disperse the veterans and their families from Washington. Tear gas was used and troops lit the shanty town that had been erected by the veterans on fire. George Patton, who like MacArthur, would later gain fame as a general in World War II, was one of the officers under MacArthur's command in Washington in the summer of 1932. There was no evidence that the veterans and civilians who gathered in the city in the spring and summer that year intended to foment violent revolution, but they were still met with overwhelming force by the Hoover administration.

A situation similar to the attack on the Bonus Army occurred in Canada in 1935 when unemployed workers in British Columbia relief camps began the On To Ottawa Trek. The federal government gradually became involved in the provision of relief as local and provincial governments came under increasing economic strain. A policy decision was made to erect work camps in remote northern regions of the country to house unemployed homeless men. The ostensible reason was to provide them with shelter and productive work, but the real purpose was to sequester the unemployed from the rest of society so that they could not become a disruptive force.

Men were not forcibly confined to the camps but lost access to any form of relief if they left them. Approximately 1,500 workers in British Columbia relief camps went on strike in May 1935 and quickly embarked on a journey to Ottawa for the purpose of compelling the government to stop punishing workers for being unemployed. The unemployed marchers made it to Regina, Saskatchewan by the end of June 1935. A small delegation of them traveled to Ottawa hoping to meet Prime Minister Bennett, but Bennett had already decided to arrest the strikers. Royal Canadian Mounted Police and Regina police began arresting striking unemployed workers on July 1, 1935.[5]

The scale of the On To Ottawa Trek and how it was stopped by the Canadian government was not equal to what happened with the Bonus

Army in the United States, but both events illustrated that national governments were not effectively grappling with the impact of the Depression. Those governments were led by conservative parties – the Conservatives in Canada and Republicans in the United States – that were closely aligned to business interests, and corporations continued their vehement opposition to public policy measures that could increase taxation and lead to wealth redistribution.

Socio-economic conditions seemed insurmountably bleak for workers in the early 1930s. The surge of union militancy that happened after World War I had been suppressed by business and government, unemployment was grievously high, and public policymakers had shown little ability to grapple with the Depression. The situation began to change in 1933 with demands for reform and greater militancy within the labor movement. The new struggle began in the AFL. The Knights of Labor were essentially a memory by the early 1930s and the IWW had been systematically attacked by the state and capital. The AFL's leadership maintained its continued hostility toward other labor federations, and still maintained a largely accommodationist stance in dealing with corporate management. The federation's leaders did not anticipate that affiliated unions would demand change.

Popular perceptions of the Depression years often lend the impression that there were more unemployed people than workers on the job. In fact, there were people working at a wide range of jobs, and workplace conditions were often poor. Corporations were well aware that they had even more power than usual in the employment relationship due to the presence of an enormous pool of unemployed workers that could be used to quickly displace employees. Work in heavy industries like automotive manufacturing, mining, and steel was often precarious and poorly paid. There were enormous gender variations in workplaces and industries as men were overwhelmingly employed in heavy manufacturing while women often predominated in the garment and textile industries.

In 1933, a movement began under the leadership of the United Mine Workers of America (UMW) to refocus the AFL's organizing efforts more fully on industrial workers. There was disagreement within the federation over which path affiliated unions should pursue, and the ultimate result was the departure of several key unions that formed the new Congress of Industrial Organizations (CIO). The CIO included the new United Auto Workers (UAW) union, the UMW, the United Steelworkers of America (USWA), and the United Rubber Workers.[6]

While historians often focus on the rise of industrial unions that were affiliated with the CIO, and on labor–management conflict in the North-Eastern industrialized states, perhaps the most consequential strike to happen in the United States in the 1930s took place in textile mills across the Southern states and East Coast. It eventually became known as the Great Textile Strike and it reflected a moment of great worker militancy and even greater employer opposition. The states of the former Confederacy never experienced industrialization to the extent found in the Northern and Mid-Western states, with the exception of developing a textile industry. The South remained largely agrarian, and its labor market continued to be predicated on sharp racial divisions including the oppression of poor whites and the terrorizing of African Americans regardless of their occupation. The prospect of workers forming a pan-racial alliance to collectively further their interests had been opposed since the Colonial period, through the Civil War and Reconstruction, and it would again be opposed when textile workers began striking in 1934.

The General Textile Strike was important because of its scope – it involved hundreds of thousands of workers from the South to the Atlantic seaboard – and because it was rooted in local labor militancy. It also mattered because it ultimately failed. Subsequent analysis will show that the South would be persistently anti-union throughout the twentieth century, which meant that a large region of the United States became essentially devoid of organized labor. While there are dangers in engaging in counterfactual historical speculation, it is nonetheless reasonable to conclude that labor conditions in the United States would have unfolded much differently from the 1930s onward had the United Textile Workers and its 300,000 members won the 1934 strike.[7]

Organized labor's defeat in the South in the 1930s was balanced with marked victories elsewhere across the United States. Most notably, members of the UAW engaged in a sit-down strike at General Motors in Flint, Michigan from 1936 to 1937 to win union recognition. There were major organizing drives by the new CIO unions, and the idea of organized labor as an influential social force entered popular consciousness. This was especially true of labor–management struggles in the automotive industry. The creation of a mass production American auto industry from the early twentieth century onward was about more than the development of enormously influential corporations. American cities were increasingly planned and built around automobile transportation and cars became cultural icons.

The United States and the National Labor Relations Act

Historian Jefferson Cowie has persuasively argued that a combination of unique social, political, and economic conditions in the United States led to the remarkable election of Franklin Roosevelt as president in 1932. Cowie convincingly suggested that immigration restrictions imposed by the 1924 Immigration Act had curbed nativist hysteria about the impact of foreign influences on American society. The power of the religious right temporarily declined by the early 1930s. The American government expanded during World War I, which gave the state a bigger role in the lives of everyday citizens. The stage was set for a more interventionist government if the people chose to elect one.[8]

The Democrat majorities in both houses of the United States Congress were enormous and afforded Roosevelt the chance to enact sweeping legislation that went beyond simply addressing the impact of the Depression and instead transformed American life. Legislation including the creation of the Social Security Administration, the National Industrial Recovery Act, the passage of the Fair Labor Standards Act, and changes to banking regulations led to an enormous expansion of the role of the federal government in the lives of average Americans. For instance, New Deal spending spurred rural electrification across the country. It was an agenda heavily influenced by the economic theories of John Maynard Keynes, who argued for a significant government role in the economy. The New Deal also transformed labor–management relations.[9]

American labor and employment law was heavily weighted toward employers rather than workers prior to the New Deal. The Railway Labor Act had been introduced in 1926 to regulate labor–management relations in the crucial rail industry but collective bargaining rights were not extended to workers across other industries.[10] Some progress began to be made in 1931 with the Davis–Bacon Act, which required payment of prevailing local wages on federal public works projects.[11] The 1932 Norris–LaGuardia Act outlawed the Yellow Dog contract which obliged workers to promise as a condition of employment that they would not join a union, placed some limits on how much employers could interfere when workers formed a union, and narrowed the scope of how courts could issue injunctions against strikes and picketing.[12] The act was a huge step forward and it would soon be followed by legislation that went even further.

In 1935, New York state senator Robert F. Wagner successfully shepherded the National Labor Relations Act (NLRA) through the United States Congress. This passage of that law marked a revolution in labor–management relations in America. It was hailed by organized labor and condemned by business. The worst economic downturn in American history had led to conditions that made it possible for American workers to engage in legal collective bargaining and form unions of their own choosing without interference from management. Collective bargaining was a new term in American workplaces. It devised by English intellectual and social reformer Beatrice Webb, one of the founders of the London School of Economics and Political Science, in 1891 and described as a process of workers collectively choosing representatives to represent them in negotiations of their employment terms and conditions.[13]

The passage of the Wagner Act is rightly described by historians as an enormous leap forward for American workers, but there are certain caveats that accompanied its passage. The Wagner Act compelled employers to engage in collective bargaining with unions that workers had freely formed, and it banned so-called company unions. Many major American corporations, such as Kodak, operated internal representation schemes that were a form of union substitution. Workers were led to believe that a pseudo union was preferable to a real one. The Wagner Act included a provision to create the National Labor Relations Board (NLRB) to oversee administration of the act, the union certification process, and resolution of complaints brought under the act. Wagner had famously said that "the right to bargain collectively is at the bottom of social justice for the worker, as well as the sensible conduct of business … the denial or observance of this right means the difference between despotism and democracy." The NLRA became commonly called the Wagner Act, and the system of labor relations that it created was similarly known as the Wagner-based system.[14]

Dispute resolution is central to the Wagner Act – its preamble into the twenty-first century affirms that it intended to foster peaceful relations between workers and employers – and that objective is pursued through the negotiation of collective bargaining agreements. A collective agreement includes articles that recognize a union as the exclusive bargaining representative for workers in a given workplace, the rights of management to run its operations (sometimes called reservation to management), wage scales, hours of work, and other articles and employment terms. A collective agreement that is up to a hundred pages is average length, but some agreements can run to many hundreds of pages in length and be highly detailed. A grievance process is usually central to any collective agreement. A grievance is a complaint lodged by a worker in response to a perceived violation of one or more of a person's rights under a collective agreement. There are usually several steps in a grievance process, and a union and an employer are supposed to at least attempt to resolve a dispute at some point in the process.

A collective agreement will also usually include an article that describes how both parties will use arbitration to resolve a dispute if it cannot be settled through the grievance process. Arbitration is a step that is distinct from the grievance process. It involves both parties in a dispute mutually agreeing on a person – an arbitrator – who will conduct a hearing in which both sides will present their arguments. An arbitrator essentially functions like a judge by hearing evidence from both sides, considering existing jurisprudence, and then issuing a written decision on a case. There is usually one arbitrator, or there is sometimes a provision for an arbitration board comprised of three arbitrators. In the latter case, one person is the union's nominee, a second is the employer's nominee, and the third person is jointly selected by the union and the employer.

Arbitration can be regarded as one of labor law's gift to the wider legal world. It eventually was used to resolve different types of business disputes and even became part of family law conflict resolution. It also brought challenges for workers along with benefits, and those aspects of it reflected wider issues with the overall Wagner framework. The Wagner Act led to the gradual creation of a vast labor law infrastructure that largely became the domain of attorneys and labor relations specialists. Universities across the United States, such as Cornell, established schools devoted entirely to the study of labor and industrial relations. Labor–management conflict became a field of serious academic inquiry.

The creation of a labor relations field of study and the development of professional expertise helped formalize labor–management interaction, and conflict between the two groups was officially channeled into legally binding dispute resolution processes. This did not mean that conflict stopped, or that it did not occasionally happen outside of the official boundaries established by the Wagner Act. Subsequent discussion will show that conflict continued to happen outside the bounds of collective bargaining. The labor relations system created by the Wagner Act led to disputes being taken out of the workplaces in which they were rooted and out of the hands of workers and managers involved in those disputes. The dispute resolution process could quickly become abstract for anyone who did not have legal training or experience as a labor relations practitioner.

The Wagner Act consequently came with benefits and limitations. It gave workers the right to unionize, and it led to a massive increase in private sector union membership in the United States. It moved labor–management conflict resolution from a system of industrial voluntarism, as exemplified by the Colorado Industrial Plan and Industrial Disputes Investigations Act (IDIA) devised by Mackenzie King, to a system of industrial pluralism. This meant moving from a system of encouraging opposing parties to negotiate to actually compel them to interact within a framework that established the legal forms of bargaining and conflict resolution. Unions became established participants in the nation's economy, and the open conflict that previously occurred somewhat abated as it was channeled into dispute resolution procedures. The limitation was that spontaneous worker action against employers was limited. The full impact of the new law would be felt as the United States entered the 1940s and fought World War II.

Canada: Wagner if Necessary but Not Necessarily Wagner

Canada entered the 1930s in dismal economic straits and the political situation changed in the country as a result of the Depression, although the policies introduced by the federal government to alleviate the country's problems were not within the scope of those implemented through the New Deal. William Lyon Mackenzie King's Liberal government was in power at the start of the Depression and lost the 1930 election as a result of an insufficiently quick response to the crisis. Losing that election was in many ways fortuitous for King. R.B. Bennett's Conservatives came into power promising to fix the nation's problems, took too long to respond, and then lost the 1935 election. King would be back in power until after World War II and became Canada's longest serving prime minister. Bennett slipped into political obscurity and was remembered as the prime minister who led Canada into the Depression, when in fact it was King who had been in office in October 1929.

King continued to obfuscate when confronting social unrest. Canada faced a crisis over military conscription in 1944 and, recognizing the sharp division over the issue between English and French Canada, King said that Canada would "have conscription if necessary but not necessarily conscription." He was equally suspicious of the New Deal, and the influence of American unions in Canada. King may have been Canada's first labor relations specialist due to his participation in crafting the Colorado Industrial Plan, but the prospect of more government involvement in labor–management relations was anathema to him. There was also the wider problem of how regulation of workplace relations would occur. The long-standing dispute between the provinces and federal government complicated the legislative response to labor–management conflict in Canada, particularly since the 1925 *Toronto Electric Commissioners v Snider* decision by the Judicial Committee of the Privy Council, which determined that the provinces would have principal jurisdiction over labor and employment legislation in Canada.[15]

There was also the fact King disliked the prospect of social conflict, and there were provincial premiers who actively fought with unions. This was especially evident in Ontario and Québec. Ontario had a Liberal government led by Mitchell Hepburn from 1934 to 1942 and he reacted to labor unrest in the same manner as his Conservative predecessors. In 1933, newly unionized workers in Stratford, Ontario – a small city that would later be principally known for its famed Shakespeare festival – went on strike to secure better wages and working conditions. The size of the city at the time and the number of workers who were on strike led the action to be called the Stratford General Strike. The federal government responded by sending two companies of troops from the Royal Canadian regiment and four tanks to the city. R.B. Bennett denied that tanks had been in the streets of Stratford, but he was obfuscating as tracked armored vehicles equipped with machine guns were deployed.[16]

Mitch Hepburn used the Stratford strike as a political bludgeon against the province's Conservative government and won the 1934 election. He did not prove to be more friendly toward organized labor than his predecessors. Mackenzie King and other Canadian politicians may have looked askance at the New Deal, but workers and unions in Canada were inspired by it. The Trades and Labor Congress of Canada was the country's main labor federation in the 1930s, and it was allied with the AFL and it continued to emphasize organizing workers on a craft rather than industry basis. CIO unions began sending organizers into Canada in the mid-1930s, which resulted in a massive expansion in unionization but also renewed conflict with employers and governments.

American auto workers had the Flint, Michigan sit-down strike in 1936 and their Canadian counterparts responded with the 1937 Oshawa General Motors (GM) strike. GM figured prominently in the formation of early labor–management relations in both the United States and Canada. Although other auto companies were the products of mergers between smaller firms, GM was created in a deliberative manner largely through the efforts of Alfred P. Sloan. Sloan wrested control of the company from its founder William Durant and revolutionized the marketing of cars. If Henry Ford made mass production of cars possible through the assembly line, Sloan transformed how they were marketed and sold.[17]

Whereas Ford said people could buy any Model T that they wanted as long as it was black, Sloan said that GM would sell a vehicle for "every purse and purpose" which meant different types of vehicles sold at different price levels. This approach eventually meant that Chevrolet would be GM's entry-level brand and eventually followed by Pontiac, Oldsmobile, Buick, and ultimately Cadillac. Sloan also introduced the idea of planned obsolescence, which involved car models being redesigned for each new year. These marketing innovations enabled GM to overtake Ford as the largest American automaker in the early twentieth century and to hold on to that distinction into the twenty-first century. GM's size and central role in the auto industry meant that it would invariably come into conflict with industrial unions.

Workers at GM's Oshawa assembly plant were already engaged in union organizing when the UAW sent money to organizers to support their strike. There is often a misconception that the workers in Oshawa sat down like their counterparts in Flint, but they did not engage in the same type of plant occupation as happened in that US city. Mitchell Hepburn was determined to keep American industrial unions out of Ontario and sent special Ontario Provincial Police constables to Oshawa to break the strike, but the UAW was still eventually able to organize the workers and it represented them in the plant for decades to come.[18]

The major American automobile companies that currently exist in the United States, with the exception of the grossly over-valued Tesla, can trace their lineages back to a collection of self-taught engineers, tremendously brash salespeople, and emerging corporate bureaucrats. Henry Ford fell into the first category. There is a debate among historians about Ford's legacy and, as Stephen Meyer noted some time ago, much of what was long thought about Ford was based on myth. The automotive assembly line devised by Ford did cut production costs and it quickly incorporated time and motion management methods championed by Taylor. Taylor's methods were also incorporated into other industries. Ford's method did lead to his first car, the Model T, being priced at such a low cost that a family living on skilled worker or middle-class wage could afford one. Ford was also the first employer in the automotive industry to willingly pay employees five dollars per day, which was an enormous daily wage for manufacturing workers. Henry Ford reasoned that he had to pay his workers enough money to purchase the products that they made. He also incessantly monitored their personal lives and absolutely hated unions.[19]

The UAW, like all CIO unions in the 1930s, devoted a majority of its resources to organizing new workplaces and it attempted to organize Ford in the mid-1930s. One particular episode chronicled on film illustrated how much hatred a major corporation could direct at organized labor during that decade. UAW president Walter Reuther and a small group of union activists that included Richard Frankensteen and Reuther's brother Victor were distributing leaflets for Ford production workers at Overpass Four at the Ford Rouge River assembly plant in Dearborn, Michigan. The Rouge plant employed close to 100,000 workers at the time and was consequently a prime organizing target for the union.

Ford employed company security staff in its Service Department who were little more than thugs and a group of them approached Reuther and his companions on May 26, 1937, as they were distributing information to workers entering the Rouge plant. A photographer from the *Detroit Free Press* was present and recorded the Ford security men attacking Reuther and his comrades. Of the group, only Richard Frankensteen attempted to fight back against Ford's thugs, who also demanded that photographer James Kilpatrick give them his film negatives. Kilpatrick hid the images that he had taken and instead handed over unused photographic plates. The photographs that he took that day caused public criticism of Ford Motor Company when they were published in the *Detroit Free Press* and were subsequently circulated around the United States. Henry Ford's carefully cultivated image as a benevolent employer was severely damaged and the union's profile was raised in public discourse.[20]

The Battle of the Overpass, as the incident at the Rouge Plant became known in labor history, was a particularly violent example of management hatred toward unions and that hatred manifested itself in other forms in the 1930s. The major American automakers were at the forefront of resistance to unions during that decade. Labor–management conflict in the 1930s generally meant interaction between corporations and private sector unions. Government workers were prohibited from unionizing and instead formed employee associations that eventually became unions. This was important because what occurred in the private sector would ultimately shape labor–management relations in the public sector. Industrial unions rose in manufacturing industries, and men were principally the workers signing union cards and most of them were white. Black workers also recognized that unionization would improve their working conditions, and Joe William Trotter has described how Black men engaged in organizing.[21]

Governments continued to be large and important employers, but existing literature on labor–management relations in the 1930s tends to emphasize developments in the private sector. Conservatives would later say that the Wagner-based system was never intended for public sector workers and that even Franklin Roosevelt had said that government workers should not have the right to unionize. The US federal government implemented regulations governing federal public employees, and eventually introduced legislation called the Classification Act in 1949 to standardize job classifications and wages across the entire federal public service, which gave workers the impression that they were being objectively treated when it came to compensation. Similar efforts to achieve uniform classification in the Canadian federal public service failed over a disagreement between governments and employee groups. Public sector workers continued to lack formal representation in the workplace with the right to collective bargaining.[22]

The 1940s: The United States

Union membership increased markedly in the United States from the passage of the Wagner Act into the 1940s. Unionization was also significantly influenced by World War II. Unions were involved in formal wartime planning to a greater extent than they were in World War I, with the understanding that leaders of national and international unions would keep their members under control and otherwise limit worker militancy. This proved difficult in practice as there were several notable strikes in both countries during the war years. For instance, the McKinnon Industries strike in St. Catharines, Ontario drew national attention because it occurred during the war.[23]

There was labor unrest in the United States during the war despite assurances from union leaders like John L. Lewis and Sidney Hillman that workers would not engage in spontaneous work stoppages. For example, there was a highly contentious strike waged by animators at Walt Disney Productions in early 1941, as the United States was anticipating entry into World War II. Workers felt emboldened because they working around the clock in an environment of labor scarcity, which meant that they were able to pursue better wages and benefit gains. There was also a return of price inflation during the war even though the American government attempted to regulate both wages and prices from 1941 to 1945. As Melvyn Dubofsky noted, there was a huge strike wave during the 12 months following the end of war.[24]

The benefits of industrial unionization were not evenly felt across the United States. Union membership was concentrated in the North-Eastern states during the 1940s, and a pattern of overall union membership being gradually concentrated in a comparatively small number of states was established for the balance of the twentieth century. Certain aspects of the Wagner Act particularly incensed politicians from the Southern states, especially provisions that gave unions security through the collection of membership dues. Business and political opposition to the rise of organized labor was often framed as a defense of personal liberty, but it was really predicated on fears that established patterns of power in the United States would be disrupted. The New Deal was hailed as a huge step forward in terms of public policy, and influences like nativism were largely forgotten or ignored by social progressives as the New Deal was regarded as a new course in American social policy and the overall direction of the country. As Kim Phillips-Fein revealed, conservatism and opposition to the New Deal persisted through the war years and it reappeared after the war ended.[25]

Democratic president Harry Truman showed less interest in running federal budget deficits than Franklin Roosevelt, and he was also increasingly concerned with the emerging Cold War with the Soviet Union. The Republican Party had been marginalized politically since 1932 – it did have strength at the state level – and it gained control of Congress in 1946. One of the first bills that the Republicans brought forward was an act jointly written by Ohio Senator Robert Taft and New Jersey Congressman Fred Hartley. Their eponymous act – the Taft–Hartley Act – amended the Wagner Act to blunt the impact of unions in American society. The law should be viewed as a product of Cold War ideology as much as latent American conservatism as it required union leaders to swear oaths they had never been Communists. This was the period of the Red Scare in the United States, and even having shown a passing curiosity in Communism was sufficient for police and politicians to wreak havoc on a person's private life.

One section of Taft–Hartley Act, 14B, had the most enduring impact on the American labor movement. That section allowed states to pass so-called Right-to-Work laws that banned agency or union shop provision in collective agreements, which in practice meant that a worker could belong to a union and enjoy protection under a collective agreement without being required to pay membership dues. Right-to-Work laws imposed a huge burden on unions as they could be obliged to represent people who did not contribute to the union's cost of representation. Right-to-Work laws were first passed in the South, beginning with Florida in 1944. Not coincidentally, the South was where the Great Textile Strike had failed to ignite a wave of permanent unionization.

The American labor movement was fractured in the late 1940s. The AFL was larger than the CIO, and it had been organizing workers by industry and not just craft since the 1930s. The CIO was still more outwardly militant, and it attempted to address the failure of the Great Textile Strike by launching an ambitious organizing drive in 1946 called Operation Dixie. The CIO made some key tactical mistakes, such as using professional organizers who were not from the South, but the full force of Southern capital and state power was marshaled to stop the organizing drive.

The 1940s: Canada

There was no legal framework in Canada to require formal collective bargaining in the late 1930s, with organized labor's legal position being as precarious as it was at the start of World War I. The federal government was keen to avoid labor disruption, even though it still happened, and it was eventually forced to implement a legal framework for collective bargaining. Taylor Hollander argues that the Canadian labor movement was aware of Wagner Act and the collective bargaining framework that it created, but that the movement felt that efforts to introduce collective bargaining were at an impasse by the late 1930s. The long-standing explanation for why Mackenzie King agreed to extend collective bargaining rights to private sector workers is that he did so because of political considerations. This is the established view among labor historians. Hollander argues that King agreed to legal collective bargaining out of principle rather than political expediency. King may have been animated by principle, but winning elections was one of his principles.[26]

A by-election in the riding of York South in Toronto in 1942. Cooperative Commonwealth Federation (CCF) candidate Joe Noseworthy defeated Conservative Arthur Meighan, who had briefly served as prime minister. The first CCF provincial government was elected in Saskatchewan in 1944 and led by Tommy Douglas. It introduced the first public health care system in the country and was a supporter of labor rights. The political environment in Canada was changing during the war years, with the CCF exerting more influence and winning elections at the national and provincial levels. King, sensing a threat to his political left, introduced Privy Council Order 1003, otherwise known as Wartime Labour Relations Regulations in order to make his government appear more allied with unions and to also alleviate social conflict. PC 1003 gave private sector workers the right to form unions of their own choosing without reprisal and engage in legal collective bargaining. In other words, the order brought the Wagner-based labor relations system to Canada. It solidified the economic and social role of organized labor in Canada, but there is a view that Wagnerism brought significant limitations for unions. For example, Cy Gonick and others argued that PC 1003 gave legal collective bargaining to unions while taking away other methods of challenging employers.[27]

A Privy Council order was an administrative edict that could be rescinded with relative ease. PC 1003 was replaced in 1948 with the Industrial Relations and Disputes Investigations Act (IRDIA), and it was successor legislation to King's pre-World War I IDIA. The IRDIA applied to federally regulated workers, and the provinces soon implemented their own versions of it. Accompanying employment standards legislation was also introduced after World War II that provided minimum working conditions for all workers, and laws like the Ontario Employment Standards Act also provided minimum terms for collective bargaining. As Mark Thomas explained, the postwar legislative framework created a divide between unionized workers who could use collective bargaining to improve their working lives, while non-unionized workers had to rely on employment standards legislation.[28]

The introduction of PC 1003 and the end of the war did not always bring labor peace in Canada. A major strike began at Ford of Canada's auto assembly operations in Windsor, Ontario over the issue of union security. All workers were covered by a collective agreement negotiated by the UAW union, yet not all of them were paying membership dues. At that time, unions had to collect dues directly from workers who were then given a lapel button, or an entry was placed in a ledger to show that they had paid their dues. The 1945 to 1946 Windsor Ford strike led to an important change in labor–management relations. The federal minister of labor appointed Canadian Supreme Court justice Ivan C. Rand to arbitrate an end to the strike, which had been highly contentious and led striking workers to use cars to blockade the factory. PC 1003 represented a concept called industrial legality, which meant what labor organizations could do within the labor–management legal framework. Rand ruled that the workplace was a form of democracy and that paying dues was required to sustain a union engaged in the representation of workers. The key idea behind this ruling was that all workers benefited from a union's representation if one was in place in their workplace and that they should all therefore contribute to it. The Rand formula became a unique feature of Canadian labor law that was not found in other countries.[29]

Politics, Labor, and Management in the 1930s and 1940s

The Rand Formula imposed some conditions on unions. They could lose union security if they violated labor law, such as going on wildcat strikes during the duration of a collective agreement. On one hand, spontaneous militancy was proscribed under a regime of industrial legality. On the other hand, spontaneous class-based militancy was dependent on the willingness of workers and their families to routinely go on strike. The labor relations framework that was built in Canada after PC 1003 became complex and navigating labor law required the help of attorneys. Labor law was a new field in the 1940s, and it began with lawyers like J.L. Cohen working with unions. The field quickly expanded in subsequent decades.[30]

Labor unrest happened across the country. The Ford strike over union security was accompanied by a strike over the same issue, along with other grievances, when workers at Asbestos, Québec went on strike in 1949. That strike was led by The Confédération des travailleurs catholiques du Canada and its legacy helped shape the Quiet Revolution in the 1960s. Québec developed its own labor movement in the 1930s and 1940s, and having English- and French-speaking labor movements was a fundamental difference between Canada and the United States.[31]

The 1930s and 1940s were pivotal decades in which workers in the United States and Canada were pushed to form unions and advance their social and economic interests. They gained a right to legal collective bargaining but it came with costs as some of organized labor's more effective measures to use against employers. This trade-off of giving up the spontaneous right to strike and engage in other forms of workplace resistance in return for legal collective bargaining through labor law is often referred to as the post-war compromise or settlement, with the implication that labor surrendered militancy without getting enough in return. The idea of a compromise between labor, capital, and the state ultimately relies on the premise that all parties involved were willing to comprise. There is little evidence that corporations in Canada were generally ready to willingly accept the legal position of unions in the workplace, which calls into question the entire idea that a compromise of any kind occurred.[32]

A similar pattern was found in the United States, at least in those states where unions were influential. As Harry A. Millis and Emily Clark Brown described, the NLRA was repeatedly challenged in court and was not declared constitutional until 1936. Even then, Robert Wagner had to link the act to the Commerce Clause in the US Conflict between labor and management became more formal and its nature shifted. Rather than send security personnel to beat union organizers, as Ford did at the Rouge Plant, management instead relied on attorneys to stop union organizing drives and politicians to block and reverse further pro-union changes to labor law. The Wagner Act did, as Richard Hurd argues, bring benefits for workers even if their liberty to resist employers was constrained by it.[33]

Table 1.1 Percentage of Employed Workers in Unions, 1930–1948

	1930	1940	1948
United States	7.5	18.3	24.5
Canada	13.1	16.3	30.3

Sources: F.H. Leacy, ed., *Historical Statistics of Canada*, second edition (Ottawa: Statistics Canada, 1938), E175–176; Gerald Mayer, "Union Membership Trends in the United States," Congressional Research Service, Library of Congress, 31 August 2004, CRS-23.

As shown in Table 1.1, there was a marked upward trend in union membership between 1930 and 1948. The membership rate in Canada increased by almost two and a half times, while the rate in the United States tripled. Canada also started with a higher unionization rate than the United States in 1930, but the impact of the Wagner-based labor relations system clearly made unions more important in the workforces of both countries. There were also key points of convergence and divergence between Canada and the United States during the 1930s and 1940s. The United States was ahead of Canada in introducing legal collective bargaining and creating a system of industrial pluralism. The purely voluntarist system was replaced by a process in which the state, capital, and labor resolved workplace disputes through formal legal structures.

Canada followed the United States within a decade, and the end of World War II proved to be pivotal for labor–management relations in both countries. Anti-communism was prevalent in both countries, although arguably more outwardly prominent in the United States, and its anti-Communism, racism, and general hostility toward unions led to anti-labor reaction exemplified in the 1947 Taft–Hartley Act. In contrast, the Rand Formula gave unions a degree of security that could not be enjoyed in Right-to-Work states. The paths taken by the two countries would eventually experience more divergence than convergence as the post-war decades unfolded.

Notes

1 Leo Panitch and Sam Gindin, *The Making of Global Capitalism: The Political Economy of American Empire* (New York: Verso, 2012), 54.
2 Eric Strikwerda, *The Wages of Relief: Cities and the Unemployed in Prairie Canada, 1929–39* (Edmonton: Athabasca University Press, 2013), 44.
3 Howard Zinn, *A People's History of the United States* (New York: Harper-Collins, 1980), 387.
4 Zinn, *A People's History,* 391.

5 Strikwerda, *The Wages of Relief,* 195–198.

6 Melvyn Dubofsky, *The State and Labor in Modern America* (Chapel Hill: University of North Carolina Press, 1994), 133–134.

7 John A. Salmond, *The General Textile Strike of 1934, from Maine to Alabama* (Columbia: University of Missouri Press, 2002), ix–x.

8 Jefferson Cowie, *The Great Exception: The New Deal and the Limits of American Politics* (Princeton: Princeton University Press, 2019), 19–21.

9 See John Maynard Keynes, *The General Theory of Employment, Interest and Money* (London: Palgrave Macmillan, 1936).

10 Dubofsky, *The State and Labor,* 100–101.

11 United States Department of Labor, "The Davis–Bacon Act, as Amended," April 2009, www.dol.gov/agencies/whd/laws-and-regulations/laws/dbra.

12 Dubofsky, *The State and Labor*, 104.

13 Virginia Doellgast and Chiara Benassi, "Collective Bargaining," in Adrian Wilkinson, et al., eds., *Handbook of Research on Employee Voice* (Cheltenham: Edward Elgar, 2014), 227.

14 Harry A. Millis and Emily Clark Brown, *From the Wagner Act to Taft-Hartley: A Study of National Labor Policy and Labor Relations* (Chicago: University of Chicago Press, 1950), 3.

15 Judy Fudge and Eric Tucker, *Labour Before the Law: The Regulation of Workers' Collective Action in Canada, 1900–1948* (Toronto: Oxford University Press, 2001), 123.

16 Stephen L. Endicott, *Raising the Workers' Red Flag: The Workers' Unity League of Canada, 1930–1936* (Toronto: University of Toronto Press, 2012), 214–215.

17 On the rise of General Motors and its relations with workers see David R. Farber, *Sloan Rules: Alfred P. Sloan and the Triumph of General Motors* (Chicago: University of Chicago Press, 2002).

18 Sam Gindin, *The Canadian Auto Workers: The Birth and Transformation of a Union* (Toronto: Lorimer, 1995), 56–58.

19 Stephen Meyer, *The Five Dollar Day: Labor Management and Social Control in the Ford Motor Company, 1908–1921* (Albany: SUNY Press, 1981), 1–2.

20 Wayne State University, "UAW – Battle of the Overpass," *Walter P. Reuther Library*, 28 April 2022, https://reuther.wayne.edu/image/tid/1203.

21 Joe William Trotter, Jr., *Workers on Arrival: Black Labor in the Making of America* (Oakland: University of California Press, 2019), 110–124.

22 Jason Russell, *Leading Progress: The Professional Institute of the Public Service of Canada, 1920–2020* (Toronto: Between the Lines, 2020), 111.

23 Pamela Sugiman, *Labour's Dilemma: The Gender Politics of Auto Workers in Canada, 1937–1979* (Toronto: University of Toronto Press, 1994), 32.

24 Dubofsky, *The State and Labor*, 193–194.

25 See Kim Phillips-Fein, *Invisible Hands: The Businessmen's Crusade Against the New Deal* (New York: W.W. Norton, 2010) for a revealing account of the rise of post-World War II business conservatism in the United States.

26 Taylor Hollander, *Power, Politics, and Principles: Mackenzie King and Labour, 1935–1948* (Toronto: University of Toronto Press, 2018), 13–14.

27 See Cy Gonick, Paul Phillips, and Jesse Vorst eds., *Labour Gains, Labour Pains: 50 Years of PC 1003* (Winnipeg: Fernwood, 1995) for analyses of the meaning of PC 1003 in the 50 years following its introduction.

28 Mark Thomas, *Regulating Flexibility: The Political Economy of Employment Standards* (Montréal and Kingston: McGill-Queen's University Press, 2009), 54–55.

29 Craig Heron and Charles Smith, *The Canadian Labour Movement: A Short History,* third edition (Toronto: Lorimer, 2020). 76.

30 For an account of the life of J.L. Cohen and the emergence of the labor law field in Canada see Laurel Sefton-MacDowell, *Renegade Lawyer: The Life of J.L. Cohen* (Toronto: Osgoode Society for Canadian Legal History, 2001).

31 Christo Aivalis, *The Constant Liberal: Pierre Trudeau, Organized Labour, and the Canadian Social Democratic Left* (Vancouver: UBC Press, 2018), 23–24.

32 See Peter McInnis, *Harnessing Labour Confrontation: Shaping the Postwar Settlement in Canada, 1943–1950* (Toronto: University of Toronto Press, 2002) for an analysis that supports the post-war compromise/settlement thesis.

33 Richard W. Hurd, "Moving Beyond the Critical Synthesis: Does the Law Preclude a Future for US Unions?" *Labor History*, 54 (2013), no. 2, 193–200.

2 The 1950s and 1960s

Many people across Canada and the United States feared the return of Depression-era economic conditions following World War II, but those fears proved unfounded. The 1950s and 1960s were a period of tremendous prosperity in both countries. There was major demographic change as Canada and the United States became two of four countries, along with the United Kingdom and Australia, to experience a post-war baby boom. The eventual entry of the baby boom generation into paid work had a profound impact on workplaces and labor–management conflict. Another major demographic change began to emerge by the end of the 1960s as women increasingly entered full-time employment. This was a 20-year period when the United States and Canada began to take increasingly divergent paths when it came to labor–management interaction. The two countries may have shared corporate employers and international unions, but important distinctions began to emerge that would become more significant as the 1960s gave way to the 1970s.

The United States in the 1950s: Industrial Pluralism, Without Radicalism

The American labor movement entered the 1950s in a seemingly strong position in American society. Sociologist C. Wright Mills wrote influential analyses of American society in the late 1940s and early 1950s, and among them was a book about labor leaders. Union leaders like the United Auto Workers (UAW)'s Walter Reuther were national media figures, and a third of the national workforce were members of unions. For the general public, the prosperous 1950s masked the tenuous position of unions in relation to management. The signs that management and labor conflict was still part of workplaces were clearly evident if people chose to look for them.[1]

DOI: 10.4324/9780429294938-3

Operation Dixie was a failure in the late 1940s, but the Congress of Industrial Organizations (CIO)'s defeat can be attributed more to the ferocity of southern opposition to unions than to tactical errors made by union organizers. The CIO unions, mainly in the textile industry, used the same tactics in the south as they had used in northern states because they worked. Critiques of Operation Dixie are prone to emphasizing the choices of the CIO and devote less consideration to the nature of southern society. Ken Fones-Wolf and Elizabeth Fones-Wolf produced one of the more insightful analyses of Operation Dixie and concluded that the CIO could not overcome anti-unionism in southern culture, especially white evangelical Protestantism, although they also note that the CIO could have done more to appeal to Black evangelical workers.[2]

Social, political, cultural, and economic conditions in the southern states were not markedly different than they had been during the Great Textile Strike, and that struggle had been largely led by southern organizers. Considerable literature has emerged in the labor studies field, such as recent work by Jane McAlevey on how to reverse declines in union membership. This includes the idea that providing workers with the resources to do their own organizing is the best method of organizing unions. Sending in professional, full-time organizers is considered an ultimately fruitless practice that will not lead to successful unionization. Using that approach to analyze events in the past reveals that the workers during the Great Textile Strike were trying to follow what is now called the organizing model, but they needed resources. The CIO indeed sent northern organizers south and did not understand Southern society and culture, but deployed resources to the region that were not there in 1934.[3]

The vociferous response of southern employers and political elites to Operation Dixie reflected management practices and beliefs that were found in other areas of the United States, but they also became dominant and manifested themselves in different ways during the 1950s. Unions represent the most visible form of class consciousness among workers because they are clearly organized to advance a collective agenda on behalf of a group of people defined by their employment status. Management also represents forms of class identity, although in somewhat more amorphous terms than what is found among working-class union members. Management, in its many forms, showed distinct hostility toward the unionized working class during the 1950s.

The 1950s mark the emergence of modern management as it can be recognized looking back from a twenty-first-century perspective. Alfred Chandler was correct in his analysis of the development of the M-form corporation, as were Adolf A. Berle and Gardner C. Means about the significance of corporations being run by managers who were not actual owners of the firms that employed them. New theories of management practice and behavior emerged in the 1950s, and they became part of a wider management sphere that assumed a prominent but often unacknowledged social role in the United States and Canada. Peter Drucker was a German-born management theorist who immigrated to the United States and exemplified the type of immigration story that is popular in American culture. He was white, smart, and European. Drucker published a book called *Concept of the Corporation* in 1946. It was a study of the internal functions of General Motors (GM), and it established him as North America's pre-eminent management thinker. Drucker became a popular media figure and would later be credited with the development of Management by Objectives.[4]

The 1950s also witnessed the beginning of the expansion of business and management education across North America. Management education had long existed in the United States and Canada, and the first undergraduate business degree had been offered in the early twentieth century. More applied management training such as basic bookkeeping had been around in the latter nineteenth century. Universities began offering Commerce degrees in both countries to provide more practical education, and also because the business community wanted to see the study of business and management elevated. There was a strong desire to make management a recognized profession equal in stature to law, medicine, and engineering. Indeed, as David Noble argued, engineering had a major role in shaping management practice in the United States and beyond.[5]

The post-World War II management edifice in the United States and Canada was comprised of people who occupied a range of roles that defined them as managers, even if they did not consider themselves equals. Whereas managerial job titles had been fairly basic prior to World War II – the industrial workplace was overseen by foremen and superintendents – managerial jobs became more varied and much of that change was due to the growth of the service sector. The growth of services was one of the defining aspects of post-war labor–management relations in Canada and the United States. Discussion of the service sector became ubiquitous as the twentieth century progressed to its end and the twenty-first century began, and the idea of that sector being a post-war creation became popular in media discourse. In reality, a service sector existed long before World War II.

The service sector comprises everything from health care to hospitality. It also includes education at its many levels, as well as finance and banking. Management was found throughout the different corners of the service sector and being a manager in a place like a retail store was a much different place on the managerial hierarchy than filling a job with the same title in a large manufacturing facility. Much of the difference in how management was perceived was rooted in gender. Manufacturing overwhelmingly employed men while the service sector tended to be predominantly female.

The common aspect of management in all sectors of the labor market in the United States and Canada was that it was overwhelmingly male. Male leadership also extended to unions with memberships that were similarly overwhelmingly female. For instance, the Amalgamated Clothing Workers of America was led by men. There were major consequences to male dominance in post-war management. From a labor–management perspective, it meant that women's issues would often get short shrift during collective bargaining. It also likely made collective bargaining more adversarial.

In terms of labor and employment legislation, the highly restrictive 1947 Taft–Hartley Act was followed by the 1959 Landrum–Griffin Act. Landrum–Griffin was a law that was devised in response to allegations that there was widespread fraud and financial mismanagement among American unions, which at that time still meant private versus public sector unions. The McClellan Committee, formally called the United States Senate Select Committee on Improper Activities in Labor and Management, met from 1957 to 1960 and was convened to investigate potential union corruption, including ties between union leaders and organized crime. As Robert Michael Smith notes, the Landrum–Griffin Act was also supposed to regulate management's use of strike-breakers and other coercive anti-union methods, but that part of the act was soon not enforced.[6]

A concerted effort to build a public narrative to oppose organized labor and the New Deal legacy was also underway by the 1950. As noted in Chapter 1, opposition to the New Deal and legislation like the Wagner Act was interrupted by World War II but resumed as soon as the war ended with the Republican Party regaining electoral ground that it lost in the 1930s. Two people, one who was principally known in business and a second who became internationally recognized for political reasons, played key roles in pushing back against the Keynesian policies of the New Deal era.

Lemuel Boulware was a vice-president at General Electric (GE), which in the 1950s was a vast and influential industrial conglomerate that manufactured an array of industrial and consumer goods. As Kim Phillips-Fein revealed, Boulware was also determined to overturn the New Deal and to take the United States on a more conservative ideological path. Boulware's name became associated with a method of collective bargaining – Boulwarism – that was entirely contrary to the idea of good faith negotiation that was supposed to be a fundamental part of the process. Boulwarism involved delivering an ultimatum to unions because Boulware believed the negotiation process to be wasteful and unnecessary. This approach to bargaining would eventually be common in the United States in subsequent years, but it is also widely considered a form of bad faith bargaining because attempting to use it means that management is not willing to engage in serious negotiations with the union opposing it.[7]

Boulware's lasting role in American politics and the rise of anti-union sentiment ran through Hollywood. In the early 1950s, Ronald Reagan was a largely unemployed B-movie actor whose best career days seemed to be largely behind him. He was also a former president of the Screen Actors' Guild, the union that represents actors and other people employed in the film and television business. Indeed, Reagan would later be the only American president to have led a union. Reagan was hired as a spokesperson for GE in 1954. He had been a New Deal Democrat, but his initial association with GE put him in Boulware's orbit and thus began his journey to the right of the political spectrum. Reagan was a far-right conservative by the mid-1960s and sought to replace Barry Goldwater as the leading right-wing voice in the Republican Party. He was twice elected governor of California during the 1960s and, while his attempts to lead his party into the White House during most of the 1970s failed, he would claim the ultimate American electoral prize in 1980. The impact of his election will form a key part of the analysis in Chapter 3.[8]

The ideological shift that began happening in sections of the American business community also began to be mirrored in higher education. Not all university faculty supported the New Deal state. As Nancy Maclean recounted, the rage that property owners across the South felt toward the New Deal and the implementation of Civil Rights legislation led to the funding of conservative academic causes that helped provide the intellectual foundations of the gradual legislative and political attack that was mounted on the New Deal order in the 1970s.[9] The 1950s witnessed the continuation of Keynesian economic policy. It was also the decade when Friedrich von Hayek's 1944 book *The Road to Serfdom* gained traction among American conservatives, von Hayek argued against government involvement in the economy and countered John Maynard Keynes.[10]

There were other groups who did not bother with intellectual pretense when opposing labor, such as when promoting the expansion of Right-to-Work laws. In that case, the National Right to Work Committee (NRTWC) is a leading example of the institutionalization of management hatred toward labor in the United States. The NRTWC was founded in 1955 to facilitate the passage of RTW laws across the country. It also funds court cases brought by individual union members who want to challenge the mandatory payment of dues. The NRTWC is just one of many advocacy groups founded in the post-war decades that either made anti-union agitation their sole policy objective or included it in a collection of other policies intended to de-regulate the American economy and otherwise strengthen the role of management and corporations.[11]

Labor, Management, and Political Economy in the 1950s

The 1950s were an economically prosperous period for most Americans, and maintaining that prosperity was a priority for policymakers. Unions won wage increases for their members that met or exceeded the cost of living, and corporations enjoyed record profits. This was the decade of the corporate conglomerate, with companies like the major automakers owning subsidiaries that seemed unrelated to their core lines of business. For instance, GM owned Frigidaire appliances. American governments at all levels expanded public infrastructure. The interstate highway system was constructed during the Eisenhower administration – ostensibly because it was needed for military purposes – and Keynesian economic thought continued to shape policy.

The ways that the labor and management chose to influence government were consistent with approaches adopted during the 1930s. American unions largely supported Democrats, although Republicans at the state and local levels occasionally received union political support, and corporate America leaned more Republican. The South was still heavily Democrat but maintaining the New Deal coalition started to become challenging in the 1950s as African Americans pressured northern Democrats to demand civil right legislation and desegregation. The American two-party political model persisted into the post-war decades, but the parties eventually evolved and shifted their power bases.

American Unions in the 1950s

Organized labor did not mount a proportional response to anti-union sentiment on the political right and the quick emergence of a growing anti-union public policy apparatus. Unions seemed strong in 1950s America, and that perception was correct. They were influential everywhere except in the South and parts of the mid-West. The socio-economic position of unions that American unions occupied in the 1950s was shaped by a key strike at the start of the decade. Unions had tried with varying enthusiasm and degrees of success to force management to agree to worker participation in the running of companies. Few ideas infuriated management more than the prospect of surrendering any control over the workplace to workers. As Howell Harris has shown, management considered the right to run organizations in an unfettered way to be a basic right that did not extend to anyone outside of managerial ranks.[12] In 1945 to 1946, UAW president Walter Reuther led a strike against GM – then the world's largest corporation – and he made a demand that GM opens its financial statements to prove that it could not meet the union's bargaining expectations. One GM executive responded that the company did not even open its books to shareholders. GM management did not agree to Reuther's demands and, in return for winning wage and benefit increases that brought middle-class incomes to blue-collar workers, the UAW gave up challenging management's prerogative to run corporations as they saw fit. The UAW later concluded a 1950 agreement with GM that became commonly called the Treaty of Detroit. The 1950 agreement led to the UAW establishing pattern bargaining with the major auto makers – Ford, GM, and Chrysler – and a type of sectoral bargaining. The gains that the union made at one company were generally accepted by the other two firms.[13]

The post-war labor relations framework channeled workplace conflict into dispute resolution mechanisms and gave unions legal recognition, but who was left out of it was as important as who operated within its parameters. The Wagner Act was initially construed by lower-level managers as giving them the right to engage in legal collective bargaining. This belief most clearly manifested itself through the formation of the Foremen's Association of America (FAA). That association was founded during World War II, and thus in the aftermath of the passage of the Wagner Act. The FAA engaged in work stoppages during the war years, with a strike at Ford's Rouge plant seeing involving 1,500 foremen. Foremen may have viewed themselves as sitting in a space between front-line workers and higher levels of management, but senior management would not accept the idea that any level of management would unionize. The FAA was opposed in the workplace, its membership was growing, and a 1947 US Supreme Court ruling involving FAA members at a Packard plant in Detroit stated that supervisors could unionize under the National Labor Relations Act (NLRA), but the Taft–Hartley Act soon prohibited managers from unionizing.[14]

The efforts of FAA members to differentiate themselves from the rest of management in their companies through unionization may seem somewhat quixotic from a twenty-first-century perspective. This is because the assumption in management thought and practice has long been that being a manager, regardless of the level occupied in an organizational hierarchy, means complete loyalty to the firm. The need for loyalty is also associated with the idea that managers can potentially have access to confidential information about a firm regardless of their rank. A more fundamental concern is how managers with supposedly divided loyalties would effectively enforce corporate policy.

One of the ironies facing front-line managers, whether they realized it or not, was that they were almost ignored in most management theories published in the post-war years. Drucker and others thought of senior executives when they defined management and, even if they did not explicitly choose to ignore front-line management, they nonetheless tended to confine people at that rank to anonymity in boxes at the bottom of organization charts. Management education began expanding in the late 1940s and into the 1950s but managing people and dealing with organized labor was not a central part of most management education programs. Management practice was divided between staff and line functions in most corporations, with areas like marketing and finance considered line areas of operation and personnel part of supporting staff areas.

Labor relations also often became called Industrial Relations (IR) during the post-war years, and it became an established field of academic study and professional practice. The scope of collective bargaining in the United States involved usual topics including wages, hours of work, vacation allotments, and benefit and pension plans. A key difference between collective bargaining in the United States and Canada, and indeed between the United States and other industrialized countries, was the centrality of employer-provided health insurance to the bargaining process. Other countries, particularly in Western Europe, introduced publicly funded healthcare systems and supplemental health insurance became a secondary bargaining item when workers participated in public healthcare plans.

American unions and employers, beginning with Kaiser shipbuilding during World War II, linked healthcare coverage to employment. This situation persisted into the 1960s with the introduction of Medicare and Medicaid by the Johnson administration, but primary health insurance coverage continued to come through employer-paid private health coverage. Health insurance eventually became a union bargaining priority equal to wages, and at times was the main issue over which employers and unions contended. Employer health insurance was intended to help keep labor peace in the United States, and to limit the role of government in healthcare provision while ensuring the growth of the private healthcare industry.[15]

The American labor movement's tactics overall became more conservative during the 1950s. The long struggle to achieve legal recognition and collective bargaining seemed to many labor leaders to have been won. The left was purged from most unions – the United Electrical Workers were an exception to that pattern – and the division between the CIO and the American Federation of Labor (AFL) ended when the two federations united in 1955 to form the AFL–CIO. Headquartered in Washington, DC, the united federation's offices at 16th Street North-West signaled to American society that the labor movement was a legitimate power broker and equal to capital. George Meany, a unionized plumber from New York City, was elected the AFL–CIO's first president in 1955. He defeated CIO and UAW president Walter Reuther, a veteran of many difficult organizing drives and rounds of negotiation, but Reuther consoled himself with the knowledge that Meany was almost a septuagenarian when elected and could not possibly stay in office for long. Reuther later died in a plane crash in 1970 while Meany stayed in office until 1979. Meany involved the American Federation of Labor and later the AFL–CIO in US government efforts to oppose left-leaning trade union movements in other countries to such an extent that the federation was sometimes derisively called the AFL–CIA, with the latter three letters referring to the Central Intelligence Agency.[16]

Canada in the 1950s: Industrial Pluralism, with Some Radicalism

The labor–management environment in Canada shared similarities with developments in the United States, but key differences in the post-war labor relations legal framework devised in the 1940s were already manifesting themselves in the 1950s. The fact that American private sector workers were covered by federal labor and employment law while Canadian private sector workers were principally covered by provincial law was a crucial difference between the two countries. The individual provinces implemented labor and employment laws that were patterned on the Industrial Relations Disputes and Investigations Act (IRDIA) described in Chapter 1. The fact that post-war private sector workers in Canada were regulated provincially rather than federally meant that unions had to be conversant with laws passed across the country, and it also shaped the potential impact of union organizing and also how labor could engage in work stoppages.

Canada had important organizing activity and labor action in the 1950s, but much of it occurred within the boundaries of specific provinces rather than becoming a cross-country labor action. In contrast, American unions could mount a massive national strike against a specific corporation and only have to satisfy regulations mandated by the Wagner Act. The experience of retail workers trying to organize at the Eaton department store chain illustrated the possibilities and limitations of post-war industrial pluralism in Canada. Eaton's, as the firm was commonly called, was a large family-owned firm that was analogous to Sears–Roebuck in the United States. Its management put up ferocious opposition when the firm's predominantly female workers tried to unionize from 1948 to 1952.[17]

Canadian employers did not always use overtly aggressive means to oppose unionization. For instance, as Robert Storey recounted, steel manufacturers Stelco and Dofasco represented a major contrast in how they handled labor–management conflict.[18] Stelco workers first unionized in 1919, and they eventually affiliated with the CIO in the late 1930s. An organizing drive began at Dofasco in 1936, and the Sherman family that owned the firm responded by firing the organizers. Dofasco management then implemented a program of welfare capitalism to instill loyalty in workers and dissuade them from again attempting to unionize. Company picnics, a wage system that mirrored those found in unionized workplaces, and other perquisites were part of welfare capitalism. As Sanford Jacoby detailed, similar systems were used on a larger scale by companies like Kodak.[19] Furthermore, as described by David Gray, the human relations school approach to motivating workers was widely used by management to make workers feel positive about their jobs and to otherwise avoid unionization.[20] Elton Mayo and Hawthorne continued to be influential.

Canadian Unions in the 1950s

Many of the contours of the modern Canadian labor movement had taken shape by the end of the 1950s. Canadian unions were shaped by the labor relations frameworks in which they operated, the industries in which they organized workers, and the wider social, cultural, and political environments in which they existed. Perhaps most importantly, Canadian unions were not essentially excluded from a region of their country unlike their American counterparts. Union density grew across Canada throughout the 1950s, with some provinces seeing larger increases than others. There was a tradition of labor activism across the country, and Canadian unions did not completely purge themselves of the political left as was done in the United States.

There was some underlying ideological conservatism among Canadian unions in the 1950s, such as within the ranks of the building trades, but industrial unions still retained activists cores that were often grounded in left politics. For instance, Walter Reuther gradually marginalized communists and other groups who were not aligned with the UAW leadership, and some efforts were made to achieve the same objective in Canada, but important Canadian UAW locals continued to include communists and socialists in their ranks. For example, UAW Local 27 in London, Ontario included communists despite the best efforts of the union's Canadian leadership to control the organization's overall agenda.[21]

The Canadian labor movement was divided into two main federations in English Canada in the 1950s: the Trades and Labor Congress and the Canadian Congress of Labor. Taking a cue from their American counterparts, the organizations merged in 1956 and became the Canadian Labor Congress (CLC). The CLC functioned much like the AFL–CIO as an umbrella organization for unions in Canada, although it did not include all unions including many in Québec. It did not directly organize workers, and instead focused on promoting a policy and political agenda across Canada.[22]

Canadian labor's involvement with electoral politics also had a profound impact on labor–management interaction in the 1950s. The Cooperative Commonwealth Federation (CCF) showed some electoral strength at the provincial level but lost traction as the decade progressed. The party never attracted a majority of unionized voters – with votes mainly being split between the Progressive Conservative and Liberal parties nationally – but the existence of a party that operated at the national and provincial levels and was oriented to the policy interests of organized labor was a major difference between how electoral politics were conducted in the United States and Canada.

The Republican and Democratic parties showed enormous animus toward third parties at the state and national levels. A de facto agreement to safeguard a two-party system was made by Republicans and Democrats. The enormous efforts that the Democrats made to marginalize successful left politicians like Vito Marcantonio – a member of the House of Representatives who was also harassed by the Federal Bureau of Investigation – illustrates the extent to which the party would not tolerate left-wing from organizations like the American Labor Party. American political parties have long been described as big tents, and the

Democratic Party included elements that liked the New Deal but were still ambivalent about unions.[23]

The CCF, even though it was a third party, occupied a different place in Canada than its American counterparts did south of the border. The party was never embraced by Canada's business class and was often criticized in corporate-owned media. The CCF was also more of an electoral threat to the Liberals than the Progressive Conservatives. It was perceived more as an English language party and had difficulty gaining traction in Québec. The CCF's base was in western Canada and ridings in industrial cities in Ontario. The party, although in need of rejuvenation by the end of the 1950s, was still a reliable ally for unions and a constant voice for worker rights.

Forming Attitudes Toward Labor in the 1950s

The importance of the Red Scare and anti-Communism in 1950s American society cannot be overstated. While popular perceptions of anti-Communist fervor, Senator Joseph McCarthy, and the House Un-American Activities Committee (HUAC) hearings tend to understandably focus on the entertainment industry, anti-Communism had a profoundly harmful impact on the American labor movement. Leftists and their allies, including people who had been members of the Communist Party of the United States of America, were purged from unions. As Judith Stepan-Morris and Maurice Zeitlin have shown, they were active members of their unions and highly effective organizers. Former and current Communists did a lot of the crucial legwork required to get cards signed and unions certified.[24]

The Kellock-Taschereau commission was somewhat equivalent to HUAC, but its impact was not as harmful or enduring. The Canadian commission met quietly, and its main impact was on federal public servants. The removal or reassignment of civil servants due to suspected communist sympathies was grievous, but it lacked the public spectacle of the HUAC hearings. Media messages in Canada supported the idea of responsible trade unionism, which meant avoiding wildcat strikes and other forms of militancy was not permitted until the system of industrial legality established through the IRDIA and its provincial equivalents.[25]

The United States in the 1960s: Radicalism, Repression, and the Start of Unravelling

The United States entered the 1960s led by a charismatic young president, John Kennedy, but this was also a period of crisis as Cold War

Table 2.1 Union Density in the United States and Canada, 1955 and 1965

	United States	*Canada*
1955	31.8 percent	33.7 percent
1965	30.1 percent	29.7 percent

Source: Leo Panitch and Donald Swartz, *From Consent to Coercion: The Assault on Trade Union Freedoms,* third edition (Aurora: Garamond, 2003), 245.

anxieties heightened. There were popular expectations that 1950s prosperity would continue into the new decade, but the United States would emerge from the 1960s much different than how it entered them. As seen in Table 2.1, union density levels in Canada and the United States were fairly equal from the mid-1950s to the mid-1960s. The United States actually had slightly higher union density in 1968, but Canadian labor gained new ground later in the 1960s while its American counterpart encountered greater hostility from management.

The position of organized labor in American society was weakened by variables that it could control and others that were beyond its influence. The industrial pluralist system brought in by the Wagner Act became more entrenched and unions continued to make significant gains through collective bargaining. The forces that were beyond labor's control began to shift in the early years of the decade. The 1960s initially seemed like they would be positive for unions. President Kennedy extended collective bargaining rights to federal public sector workers in 1962 through executive order 10988.[26]

Kennedy's order led to a substantial increase in the number of federal workers who belonged to unions. The order did not grant federal workers the right to strike. While there was Congressional oversight of federal labor–management relations, it was not common for Congress to become directly involved in federal public sector collective bargaining matters. Federal agencies engaged in bargaining and Congress was apprised of how issues progressed. The main legacy of Executive Order 10988 was that it led to the extension of collective bargaining rights to public sector workers in several states, although a patchwork system developed as many states – again in the Right-to-Work south – severely limited the scope of public sector collective bargaining.

The growing influence of the Civil Rights movement had an ancillary impact on labor–management relations. Most unions had not proven adept at organizing African-American workers and, with the exception of the Brotherhood of Sleeping Car Porters, there were no major majority African-American unions.[27] The famed 1963 March on Washington led by Martin Luther King Jr. – which was more fully known as the March on Washington for Jobs and Freedom – received significant funding from organized labor. Walter Reuther was on stage with King because the UAW had helped make the march happen.[28] The American labor movement supported the passage of the 1964 Civil Rights Act, which had a significant impact on employment through initiatives such as Affirmative Action.

Much of the social unrest in the United States during the 1960s and early 1970s was related to American involvement in the Vietnam War. Differing social views on the conflict spilled into public view in an event that happened immediately after the 1960s. A 1970 event that came to be called the Hardhat Riot exemplified the class conflict that was aggravated during the 1960s. David Kuhn recently recounted events that led to an open fight between student demonstrators and construction workers in New York City on May 8, 1970. Only four days earlier, on May 4, 13 students were shot and four killed at Kent State University in Ohio while protesting the war in Vietnam. They had been shot by Ohio national guardsmen. The demonstration four days later in New York City was part of student strike in response to the events at Kent State and the thousand students engaged in it were attacked by a mob of 400 construction workers. It was an open and violent class conflict and such social divisions further weakened labor's ability to confront management, and more conflict was coming.[29]

The Post-War Order Starts Coming Apart

Labor studies academics often point to the 1970s as the turning point for the New Deal Era – and it would prove to be a difficult decade for unions when facing management – but the roots of the shift in labor–management conflict are found in places where organized labor was not paying close attention. The first two decades after World War II were utterly dominated economically by the United States to an extent that would seem remarkable by twenty-first-century standards. Wall Street had an absolute stranglehold on global finance, the United States dollar was the strongest currency and, most importantly, the United States did not have viable international economic competitors in the 1950s. American media and culture were extending around the globe through the 1950s. America's two principal wartime opponents, Japan and West Germany, became its post-war military allies and they were quickly becoming economic competitors by the mid-1960s.

American union leaders thought a lot about pension plans – they devoted considerable time to win them at the bargaining table – but there is little evidence that they were aware of changes in global financial markets or fully grasped the implications of growing international economic competition. One of the most notable was the rise of the Eurobond. American law stipulated that trade in US-denominated securities had to be conducted by US banks. This help explains their enormous influence on global financial markets. European financiers chafed against US dominance and the Eurobond was devised by London bankers S.G. Warburg to get around financial regulation and taxation. The bond was first issued in 1963, was denoted in US dollars, and was initially traded from Luxembourg. It represented yet another crack in US economic hegemony. Another less evident but even more worrisome trend appeared in 1965. The post-war economy still seemed to be experiencing runaway growth, but growth had in fact begun to slow. Corporate profits began to lessen, which in turn altered management views on corporate planning. Unions were still winning wage increases that exceeded inflation, but management started thinking about rolling back labor's collective bargaining gains.[30]

American Public Sector Unionization

American union density began declining in the late 1960s, but it was less because of actual losses of unionized jobs and more due to the fact that the labor force was growing but not unionizing at the same rate. It would have looked even more parlous by the 1960s had it not been for greater militancy among public sector workers, which was on ample display by the latter years of the decade. Teachers and municipal workers were often at the forefront of labor action in the 1960s American public sector, and state governments such as New York's responded with legislation.

The New York State government, in which the Republican Party was strong, did not respond to public sector militancy by trying to attack unions. New York historically had high union density and many union members voted Republican. The state governor in 1967, Nelson Rockefeller, instead established a commission to look at legislative options to create a more comprehensive public sector labor relations framework. The state's first public sector labor law had been passed in 1947, also under a Republican governor, and Rockefeller's move to update the law seemed timely. The Taylor Law, as the 1967 Public Employees Fair Employment Act was commonly called, banned strikes and lockouts, did not mandate any form of arbitration for most public workers in the event that two parties engaged in bargaining could not conclude an agreement, and established the Public Employment Relations Board to enforce the law and adjudicate improper practice disputes. The Taylor Law was actually progressive compared to the labor laws passed in many American states in the 1960s.[31]

American Unions and Employers in the 1960s

The US Labor Movement became even more ideologically conservative in the 1960s than it had been in the preceding decade. Public sector workers began taking more prominent roles in the movement and were more frequently challenging management. The dual role of the government as employer and legislator came into focus as governments passed laws that gave legislatures and bureaucracies disproportionate power in the labor–management relationship. Some public sector unions that gained collective bargaining rights, even if limited, eventually became enormously influential. Elementary and high school teachers would greatly expand their influence through membership in the American Federation of Teachers and the National Education Association. Police unions, more formally called benevolent associations, also became powerful and controversial.

Private sector unionization did not become entirely devoid of militancy during the 1960s. Building trades unions showed militancy, although they were principally focused on economic gains and health and safety issues. Rank-and-file industrial union members continually challenged management on shop floors which, as Jeremy Milloy has revealed, were often rife with violence.[32] Management began to be concerned with profitability although was not yet fully attuned to the potential threat of foreign competition at home and abroad. Corporations were determined that unions would not expand beyond the industries that they organized in the 1930s, and the experience of California migrant workers demonstrates the extent to which management opposed efforts by even the poorest workers to make gains through collective bargaining. As Marshall Ganz revealed, migrant farms workers were usually Latino and often undocumented, and they successfully challenged California fruit and vegetable growers and won the passage of legislation that gave farm workers the right to unionize.[33]

The United Farm Workers (UFW) struggle brought new leadership into the wider labor movement as the union was led by Cesar Chavez, Dolores Huerta, and others. The AFL–CIO once again did not uniformly stand behind the UFW, but some unions such as the UAW offered support. The farm workers struggle was important because the NLRA did not cover agriculture and other sectors of the labor force such as housekeepers. This was deliberately to keep wages in those sectors low, and they were also areas of the economy that predominantly employed workers of color. The racial and gender biases built into the Wagner Act framework persisted into the 1950s and 1960s, and American employers were uninterested in seeing the system change.

Canada in the 1960s: Radicalism, Unrest, and New Unionization

Social, economic, cultural, and political trends in Canada shared some similarities with the United States in the 1960s but there were also major areas of divergence. Canada was pressured by the Johnson administration to become an active participant in the Vietnam War but declined. The country became more economically linked to the United States, especially following the conclusion of the 1965 Auto Pact, which was formally called the Canada–United States Automotive Products Agreement. That agreement required American automakers to build as many cars in Canada as they sold there. It greatly strengthened the Canadian auto sector and helped expand other industrial sectors such as steel manufacturing. The problem was that the manufacturers building cars in Canada were American, and the trend of Canada being a branch plant economy was reinforced.[34]

The branch plant model did not extend to all industries in Canada, with natural resource extraction and processing continuing to feature large domestic firms such as those in pulp and paper and mining. Those industries were often unionized. Other key sectors of the Canadian economy were devoid of unionization due to determined opposition to worker organization. Banks and insurance companies were example of sectors that continually opposed unionization. The overall effect was to confine private sector unionization to certain areas of the economy.

The emphasis that many unions placed on making material gains through collective bargaining represented a business unionism rather than social unionism policy approach. Whereas social unionism frames organized labor as a movement for social change as well as a bargaining representative in the workplace, business unionism is principally about more bread and butter for workers. Some industrial unions in the 1950s and 1960s, such as the UAW, moved toward a social unionism model. Others, such as those in the construction trades, generally adhered to a business unionism approach when devising policy. Public sector unions had yet to expand but would more closely adhere to the social unionism model in the 1970s and beyond.[35]

Canadian industrial unions had not yet expanded their internal structures to employ large numbers of people, but they had still become employers. They began employing full-time staff representatives in the 1930s and an increasing emphasis on business unionism in the 1960s preoccupied many union leaders. Tangible collective bargaining gains were made in the 1960s as wage increases met or exceeded the cost of living, Canadian employers resisted unionization but did not create an extensive anti-union lobbying apparatus such as the one that existed in the United States. There was no Canadian analog to the National Right to Work Committee.

The major political parties did not oppose labor in the 1960s to the extent found in the United States. The CCF was reconstituted in 1960 and became the New Democratic Party (NDP). That effort was largely led by the CLC, and it brought the labor movement much more into electoral politics. The new party would never capture a majority of the unionized vote in Canada, but it consistently received material support from unions and benefited from the work of rank-and-file union activists who came out in droves to work on NDP election campaigns.

There were left and right wings within the Progressive Conservative and Liberal parties, but nothing equal to the division that existed within the Democratic Party over labor rights. The Progressive Conservatives still included a so-called Red Tory wing that was socially progressive, much as the Republicans still had some liberals in their own ranks. The importance of having the NDP sitting in Canada's parliament became evident when the Liberals returned to power in 1963. They were able to form a minority government with NDP support and held power with NDP support in 1965. The Liberals, facing pressure from New Democrats, introduced the Canada Pension Plan, universal public care, and extended collective bargaining rights to federal public sector workers. Those measures were met with resistance from the business community, and they represented a left-ward shift in Canadian public policy.

Management education and training on labor–management relations usually occurred through workplace seminars rather than in university undergraduate and graduate business programs. The creation of community colleges across Canada in the late 1960s expanded post-secondary education, including management education. The general perception across Canada is that community colleges were initially founded with a focus on vocational training, but educating front-line management was also part of their curriculums from their inception.[36]

Labor–management relations in Canada continued to be profoundly impacted by the creation of English and French language systems. Québec was the most ideologically conservative province in the country and culturally distinct up until 1960. A Liberal government led by Jean Lesage was elected and began implementing policies collectively called the Quiet Revolution. The Asbestos Strike described in Chapter 1 helped set the stage for enormous social and cultural change in Québec. Québeckers wanted to be "maître chez nous," meaning masters in their own house. The Québec labor movement was already unique compared to other provinces because it was home to unions that were affiliated with the Catholic Church. Its distinctiveness continued into the 1960s with only one of the province's labor federation – the Québec Federation of Labor/Fédération des travailleurs et travailleuses du Québec – being formally allied with the CLC.

Canadian Public Sector Unionism

The different trajectory of its public sector unionism differentiated Canadian labor–management relations from the United States more than any other development since the end of World War II. There were employee associations throughout the federal, provincial, and municipal public sectors across Canada by the mid-1960s. The extension of formal collective bargaining rights to public sector workers is often believed to have been a result of labor militancy during a 1965 postal strike. In fact, the idea of introducing formal collective bargaining in Canada was under active consideration in Ottawa beginning with the 1963 Preparatory Committee on Collective Bargaining. Federal employee associations were obviously aware of collective bargaining, but they did not uniformly endorse the prospect of adapting the Wagner-based system to the public service. The Whitley Council model was still exemplified at the federal level through the National Joint Council and it importantly showed that pre-Wagner British influence was still found in Canadian labor relations.[37]

The Pearson government passed the Public Service Staff Relations Act (PSSRA) in 1967 with the support of the NDP. The act revolutionized federal public sector workplace representation. The many employee associations that were mostly run by volunteers and ran on usually meager budgets quickly certified as unions under the act. Their organizational structures grew, they hired staff, and their financial resources vastly increased as they were able to collect mandatory dues or fees in lieu of dues. The provinces later implemented labor laws that extended collective bargaining rights to public employees, but those laws were not closely patterned on the federal model. For instance, Ontario passed a range of laws that variously covered provincial employees, community colleges, and police and protective services. Mandatory arbitration of collective agreements that could not be concluded through regular bargaining became a key aspect of public sector bargaining that emerged in Canada starting in the late 1960s. For instance, legislation that would eventually cover police services at the municipal level made it possible for police associations to request arbitration to settle collective bargaining disputes once first negotiating with local police service boards. This was to compensate for the inability of many public sector workers, such as those in protective services and health care, to go on strike.

Canadian Unions and Employers in the 1960s

Canadian unions and employers confronted each other across bargaining tables and on picket lines in the 1960s. The idea of a postwar concordat whereby both sides accepted the parameters of industrial legality is questionable. Unions and their members continually filed grievances and brought them to arbitration, and management relentlessly sought to expand its right to run organizations in an unfettered manner. One of the most notable aspects of collective agreements is the union recognition and management rights clauses (sometimes called reservation to management). Union recognition clauses are usually not lengthy and confirm a union's role as the exclusive bargaining representative in a workplace and also include language on collection and remittance of dues. Management rights clauses became lengthier and more detailed as the post-war decades passed, and essentially said that management could run an organization as they saw fit unless something in a collective agreement stipulated otherwise. The public sector collectively gradually became the largest unionized employer in Canada following the introduction of the PSSRA in 1967. A similar process also unfolded in the United States, but the trend was much more profound in Canada.

The Cusp of Change

Labor and management in Canada and the United States ended the 1960s in a period of prosperity that had endured since the end of World War II. Collective bargaining was enshrined in law and supported by courts. Employers, especially in the American South, maintained their historic hostility toward unions but labor appeared to have become an established social institution. American unions did not benefit from an alliance with a social democratic party like the NDP, but they were closely allied with the Democrats and there were even some Republicans who wanted to promote collective bargaining. Conditions in both countries were about to change.

Notes

1 C. Wright Mills, *The New Men of Power: America's Labor Leaders* (New York: Harcourt, Brace & Co., 1948).

2 Elizabeth Fones-Wolf and Ken Fones-Wolf, *Struggle for the Soul of the Postwar South* (Urbana: University of Illinois Press, 2015), 6–7.

3 See Jane McAlevey, *No Shortcuts: Organizing for Power in the New Gilded Age* (New York: Oxford University Press, 2016).

4 Peter Drucker first outlined Management by Objectives in *The Practice of Management* (New York: Harper and Brothers, 1954).

5 See David Noble, *America by Design: Science, Technology, and the Rise of Corporate Capitalism* (Oxford: Oxford University Press, 1977).

6 Robert Michael Smith, *From Blackjacks to Briefcases: A History of Commercialized Strikebreaking and Unionbusting in the United States* (Athens: Ohio University Press, 2003), 102.

7 Kim Phillips-Fein, *Invisible Hands: The Businessmen's Crusade Against the New Deal* (New York: W.W. Norton, 2010), 97.

8 Phillips-Fein, *Invisible Hands*, 112.

9 Nancy MacLean, *Democracy in Chains: The Deep History of the Radical Right's Stealth Plan for America* (New York: Penguin, 2017).

10 Friedrich Von Hayek, *The Road to Serfdom* (Chicago: University of Chicago Press, 1944).

11 National Right to Work Committee, "About the National Right to Work Committee," 30 April 2022, https://nrtwc.org/about-the-national-right-to-work-committee/.

12 Howell John Harris, *The Right to Manage: Industrial Relations Policies of American Business in the 1940s* (Madison: University of Wisconsin, 1982) is still a well-regarded analysis of management ideology and interaction with workers.

13 See John Barnard, *American Vanguard: The United Auto Workers During the Reuther Years, 1935–1970* (Detroit: Wayne State University Press, 2004), 208–219 for an account of the legacy of the 1945–1946 GM strike.

14 On the Foreman's Association of America see Charles P. Larrowe, "A Meteor on the Industrial Relations Horizon: The Foreman's Association of America," *Labor History*, 2 (1961), no. 3, 259–294.

15 Thomas A. Kochan, Adrienne E. Eaton, Robert B. McKersie and Paul S. Adler, *Healing Together: The Labor–Management Partnership at Kaiser Permanente* (Ithaca: Cornell ILR Press, 2009), 25–33. The Kaiser name is

now associated with the Kaiser Permanente health-care system and its affiliation with shipbuilding is largely forgotten.

16 On the overseas activities of the AFL–CIO see Tony Carew, *American Labour's Cold War Abroad: From Deep Freeze to Détente, 1945–1970* (Edmonton: Athabasca University Press, 2018). New York: Free Press, 1978.

17 See Eileen Sufrin, *The Eaton Drive: The Campaign to Organize Canada's Largest Department Store, 1948 to 1952* (Toronto: Fitzhenry and Whiteside, 1982).

18 Robert Storey, "The Struggle to Organize Dofasco and Stelco," *Industrial Relations/Relations Industrielles* 42 (1987), no. 2, 366–383.

19 On Kodak see Sanford Jacoby, *Modern Manors: Welfare Capitalism Since the New Deal* (Princeton: Princeton University Press, 1997), 57–95.

20 David Gray, *Work Better, Live Better: Motivation, Labor, and Management Ideology* (Amherst: University of Massachusetts Press, 2020), 162–184.

21 Jason Russell, *Our Union: UAW/CAW Local 27 from 1950 to 1990* (Edmonton: Athabasca University Press, 2011), 5.

22 Craig Heron and Charles Smith, *The Canadian Labour Movement: A Short History,* third edition (Toronto: Lorimer, 2020), 87.

23 Gerald Meyer, *Vito Marcantonio: Radical Politician, 1902–1954* (Albany: State University of New York Press, 1989).

24 Judith Stepan-Morris and Maurice Zeitlin, *Left Out: Reds and America's Industrial Unions* (Cambridge: Cambridge University Press, 2002) is an insightful account of leftists in unions.

25 Reg Whittaker and Gary Marcuse, *Cold War Canada: The Making of a National Insecurity State, 1945–1957* (Toronto: University of Toronto Press, 1994), 57–58.

26 Richard Kearney, *Labor Relations in the Public Sector,* fourth edition (New York: CRC Press, 2009), 14.

27 Working conditions for sleeping car porters, all of whom were African American, were abysmal. For an account see Alan Derickson, "'Asleep and Awake at the Same Time': Sleep Denial Among Pullman Porters," *Labor: Studies in Working-Class History of the America's,* 5 (2008), no. 3, 13–44.

28 Erik Loomis, *A History of America in Ten Strikes* (New York: The New Press, 2018), 160.

29 For an incisive account of the Hardhat Riot see David P. Kuhn, *The Hardhat Riot: Nixon, New York City, and the Dawn of th.e White Working-Class Revolution* (Oxford: Oxford University Press, 2020).

30 Chris O'Malley, *Bonds without Borders: A History of the Eurobond Market* (Chichester: Wiley, 2015), 24.

31 John F. Wirenius, "Introduction," John F. Wirenius, ed., *The Taylor Law at 50: Public Sector Labor Relations in a Shifting Landscape* (Albany: New York State Bar Association, 2019), 3–6.

32 Jeremy Milloy, *Blood, Sweat, and Fear: Violence at Work in the North American Auto Industry, 1960–1980* (Vancouver: UBC Press, 2017) is an insightful and troubling account of working conditions in North American auto plants.

33 Marshall Ganz, *Why David Sometimes Wins: Leadership, Organization, and Strategy in the California Farm Worker Movement* (Oxford: Oxford University Press, 2009) is one of the better analysis of the rise of the United Farmworkers (UFW) union.

34 On the creation of the Auto Pact see Dimitry Anastakis, *Auto Pact: Creating a Borderless North American Auto Industry, 1960–1971* (Toronto: University of Toronto Press, 2005).

35 On social unionism see Stephanie Ross, "Varieties of Social Unionism: Toward a Framework for Comparison," *Just Labour* 11 (Autumn 2007), 16–34.

36 See Jason Russell, *Making Managers in Canada, 1945–1995: Companies, Community Colleges, and Universities* (New York: Routledge, 2020).

37 Jason Russell, *Leading Progress: The Professional Institute of the Public Service of Canada, 1920–2020* (Toronto: Between the Lines, 2020), 19.

3   The 1970s and 1980s

Workers and employers in Canada and the United States entered the 1970s anticipating that the coming decade would be much like the one that preceded it. The societies of both countries were changing, but the general expectation was that the post-war economic expansion would continue, even though profits had begun to decline in the mid-1960s. Organized labor was shaped by a range of economic, social, political, and cultural factors as it had always been, but divergence between the union movements in both countries accelerated in the 1970s before reaching a breaking point in the 1980s. The post-war consensus, which was already a tenuous concept, came to an end during the 1970s.

A new decade obviously begins with two new digits added to the end of a year, but the 1970s really began for organized labor and corporate management in 1973. There was ongoing social and political change in Canada and the United States, but major economic change had yet to occur in 1970. Canada experienced the October Crisis in 1970s, which involved the invocation of the War Measures Act in response to terrorist activity by the Front de libération du Québec (FLQ) in Québec. The act was also used to harass leftist activists across Canada. Prime Minister Pierre Elliot Trudeau, who had been considered a friend of organized labor in earlier years, was revealed to have hardline tendencies when it came to protecting social order. Unions would see how punitive he could be toward them later in the decade.

The labor movement felt the impact of economic and political change but did not grasp the extent of the changes that occurred in the business community. Management became more sophisticated and aggressive in the 1970s, especially in the United States. Collective bargaining became increasingly politicized as the business community actively sought to restrict union activity, while also pursuing the implementation of policies that harmed workers. The main political parties in both the United States and Canada, with the exception of the New

DOI: 10.4324/9780429294938-4

Democratic Party (NDP), showed less interest in workers' issues than they had from the 1940s to the 1960s. The 1970s and 1980s were pivotal decades during which labor often came under different forms of attack from management.

The United States in the 1970s

In economic terms, the 1960s ended and the 1970s began in 1973 and it was because of events that were really beyond the control of workers in Canada or the United States. The United States provided military support to Israel during the Yom Kippur war, and the Organization of Petroleum Exporting Countries (OPEC) responded by initiating an oil embargo. The OPEC embargo changed the balance of power in the global oil industry as national governments in petroleum exporting countries gained greater control over oil pricing at the expense of the major petroleum companies. The embargo also initiated an era of so-called stagflation in the United States and to a lesser extent Canada as prices increases while economic growth remained stagnant compared to what had been experienced from the late 1940s to the 1960s.

The change in economic environment in the 1970s was an enormous adjustment for labor and management. There were sectors of the Canadian and American economies that were particularly impacted, especially the automotive industry. Automotive was still dominated by the three Detroit-based automakers in the 1970s, and they attempted to adjust to the OPEC embargo and increases in the price of gas by introducing new models that were smaller and intended to be more fuel-efficient. GM, Ford, and Chrysler were beginning to pay attention to Japanese competition by the mid-1970s, mainly because Japanese cars were more fuel efficient, and also had better build quality.

Many Canadian and American products were poorly made compared to their Japanese equivalents and the work processes and labor relations behind them were dismal. Conditions in early 1970s factories were often tense, with clashes between management and unions and within unions. This was clearly seen at the General Motors (GM) plant in Lordstown, Ohio, where a major wildcat strike occurred in 1972. That plant manufactured a range of GM products from 1966 to 2019, and it was widely known as a hotbed of union militancy in the 1970s. A highly regimented management style had little appeal for young baby boom workers who joined rather than formed the UAW. Whereas the World War II generation mainly proved willing to accept regimentation of the industrial workplace in return for receiving middle-class wages and benefits, the baby boomers were much less willing to do so.[1]

American Unions in the 1970s

The American labor movement entered in the 1970s in a less powerful position than it was in 1960. The movement had been largely purged of its left-leaning members and its leadership did not often demonstrate much willingness to confront management. Rank-and-file union members and local activists did act militantly, in both the public and private sectors. One of the more notable examples of public sector labor unrest happened in 1970 with a strike by American postal workers. The post office is an integral part of public infrastructure in most countries, and the US Post Office was a key component in public communication.

Philip F. Rubio recently analyzed the eight-day strike that postal workers mounted. The US Post Office was a government department and, while workers were organized into nine different unions across the country, they did not have full collective bargaining rights. The strike was an illegal wildcat walkout. Rubio argues that the end result of the strike was to force the federal government to accept legal collective bargaining for postal workers. The Nixon administration passed a Postal Reorganization Act following the strike, workers received a 14 percent wage increase, and the post office became the US Postal Service and thereafter functioned as a stand-alone public entity responsible to Congress and the Executive Branch.[2]

The purpose and direction of American organized labor in the 1970s has been the subject of some debate among historians. The US underwent significant cultural change during the decade as the working class came under increasing threat from corporations and right-wing politicians. Jefferson Cowie argues that the 1970s were a period of crisis and decline for blue-collar workers. They were still mostly Democrats but felt under siege and responded accordingly. Cowie notes that strike action peaked in 1970 to an extent not seen since 1946.[3]

There were still some efforts made by both political parties to appeal to working-class voters and gain favor with organized labor. The Nixon administration proved to be challenging for Democrats and their labor allies. Richard Nixon was a political outsider and politically astute despite his role in the 1973 Watergate scandal. He and his advisors pursued a "blue-collar" strategy to leverage working-class voters away from the New Deal coalition.[4] That strategy involved appealing to feelings of white working-class grievance – such as railing against liberal elites – while also implementing policy changes that appealed to working-class voters. Nixon signed the Occupational Health and Safety Act in 1970, which extended long-sought workplace health and safety protection to workers. As Cowie noted, that act linked directly to Nixon's efforts to appeal to white working-class voters.[5]

The Democratic policy response to Nixon was not especially effective. The Humphrey–Hawkins Full Employment Bill is a leading policy example of Democratic policy challenges in the 1970s that related to the workplace. The act was designed to provide full employment through government policy intervention, which was also a long-sought objective for many people in the labor movement. Richard Nixon resigned in disgrace in 1973 because of Watergate, and Vice-president Gerald Ford became president. Ford lost the 1976 election to southern Democrat Jimmy Carter, and the Humphrey–Hawkins bill seemed to have a new lease on life with a Democratic president back in the White House. As Cowie reveals, Carter's advisors did not support the idea of government implementing specific policy measures to ensure full employment, and in fact many of them preferred to let the free market determine how employment functioned in the United States.[6] A watered-down version of it was passed in 1978, but it was ultimately a policy failure.

While Cowie emphasizes working-class decline during the 1970s, and points to events such as the failure of the Humphrey–Hawkins Act, Lane Windham takes a markedly different perspective on what happened during that decade. She noted that American workers continued to vote in National Labor Relations Board (NLRB) union certification elections at the same pace that they did during the 1950s and 1960s.[7] Windham attributes the decline of unions to global economic change that accelerated during the 1970s and says that Cowie's assertions about the decline of worker militancy are incorrect.[8] She describes the successful 1978 organizing drive at Newport News Shipbuilding as an example of enduring worker militancy during the 1970s.[9]

Union density declined during the 1970s, and the composition of the labor movement altered. Public sector unionization expanded during the 1970s, and legislation was actually passed in Congress and signed by Jimmy Carter that codified bargaining rights initially granted by John Kennedy's Executive Order 10998 and Richard Nixon's Executive Order 11491. The 1978 Civil Service Reform Act specified how organizing would take place, outlined unfair practices, and established a grievance and arbitration process. The act additionally created the Federal Labor Relations Authority. It also prohibited mandatory union dues collection, which entrenched Right-to-Work at the federal level and prohibited federal public sector workers from striking. The act also gave a president considerable discretion when it came to directing collective bargaining processes in the federal public service. The public sector bargaining environment at the state level continued to show considerable variation, with only Montana permitting public sector workers to go on strike. The Civil Service Reform Act represented a limited success for public sector unions, but a relatively moderate Labor Law Reform Act introduced in 1977 to modernize aspects of the National Labor Relations Act was stopped by Republican opposition in Congress.[10]

The labor movement disapproved of more open immigration, fearing more competition for work, but the Johnson administration's 1965 Immigration and Nationality Act (also called Hart–Cellar) led to a transformation of the workforce as people began to arrive from countries other than those in Europe. Forming organizing coalitions of workers with different racial and ethnic backgrounds was possible, as Windham argues, but a lot of unions were reluctant to attempt it. The structural economic changes of the 1970s that both Cowie and Windham describe were significant factors in union decline during the 1970s, and those changes were assiduously exploited by management.

American Management in the 1970s

Workers and their unions were under attack during the 1970s, and employers were much more united and engaged in directing the attacks. The economic system created during the immediate post-World War II years began to seriously disadvantage American workers following 1973. A recession occurred in 1975 and unemployment increased as a result. American employers already enjoyed enormous control over workplaces and they were determined to shift away from the post-war labor relations model that so many of them already disliked. As Mel Van Elteren notes, managers and corporations became more politically active. For instance, the Business Roundtable was founded in 1973 and its membership comprised the hundred largest companies in the United States. Forcing an anti-union agenda was part of wider corporate policy.[11]

Management learned from its conflicts with unions during the pre-Wagner Act decades. Images of company security staff beating picketing workers reflected poorly on a corporation's image. This did not mean that management would not force a strike or lockout workers, and instead meant that less overtly coercive measures could be used to frustrate unions and even avoid unionization. For example, management publications in the 1970s started talking about a "new non-union model" for organizations that included good compensation, a strong internal culture, an active human resources department, and the use of union-avoidance consultants in the event that management faced an organizing drive. This approach involved re-introducing much of what firms like Kodak had already tried in earlier decades, but it seemed novel in the 1970s.[12]

The last detail – hiring consultants to stop organizing drives – became extremely popular with managers in many firms. Such a person was often employed in a law or consulting firm that ostensibly specialized in labor and employment law. Martin Levitt was one such person and became so disgusted with the work that he spent decades doing that he wrote a memoir about it. Union avoidance strategies involved measures like holding captive audience meetings in which workers were cautioned about the alleged perils of joining a union. Being "union free" was portrayed as a virtue for workplaces. Union avoidance campaigns usually involved threats to close workplaces, and the illegal firing of workers involved with running organizing drives.[13]

Managers and politicians in the southern states maintained steadfast opposition to unionization during the 1970s. They often argued that unions would be an unwelcome third party in a workplace, without realizing that a union is comprised of workers. This opposition sometimes made it into popular media, with the experience of textile worker Crystal Lee Sutton being one of the more notable examples. Sutton was a single parent working at a textile mill owned by J.P. Stevens in 1973. The mill was located in Roanoke, North Carolina. Working conditions in the mill were unsafe and workers were poorly treated. Sutton became heavily involved in an organizing drive that led to the Amalgamated Clothing and Textile Workers being certified as the bargaining representative at the mill. Sutton's experience with the organizing drive was the basis of the film *Norma Rae* starring Sally Field.[14]

The success of organizing drives declined during the 1970s as management engaged in ever more aggressive behavior when workers tried to unionize. That behavior was also on display during negotiations to renew collective agreements. Another major problem facing organized labor was the reality that jobs were being created in industries that were not easily unionized. Companies associated with advanced technology, such as International Business Machines, assiduously opposed unionization. A new post-war professional and technical class developed across the United States, and unions either did not have success organizing them or did not bother trying despite having some organizing success during World War II. Unions of professional and technical workers were concentrated in the public service and rarely found in corporations.[15]

Canada in the 1970s

Canada entered the 1970s facing some of the same challenges prevalent in the United States. The country was divided geographically and politically as the western provinces, especially Alberta, became disenchanted with federal economic policy. The Liberal Party governed the country for most of the decade, with the exception of a few months following a federal election in 1979. The global economic challenges that confronted American labor and management were also found in Canada, although with some key differences such as the impact of deindustrialization. Deindustrialization means the loss of manufacturing facilities and jobs, often to other countries. William Adler quite succinctly describes the American deindustrialization experience by looking at the loss of jobs in a New Jersey electrical components factory.[16] The jobs first went to a new plant in the Mississippi – the factory owners had been wooed by Mississippi politicians and business interests with the promise that their state was union free – then from Mississippi to Mexico. Jefferson Cowie recounted a similar process by looking at the movement of jobs at Radio Corporation of America (RCA).[17] Mexico established the Maquiladora zone as a place to attract foreign investment, and the Mexican government succeeded. Volkswagen was the first major foreign automaker to open a plant in Mexico in 1967.[18] It was soon followed by other manufacturers.

Canada did not deindustrialize like the United States during the 1970s. There was considerable concern within the labor movement about holding on to manufacturing jobs. Some factories closed during the 1970s, but others opened. The presence of the Auto Pact had a positive impact on automotive manufacturing in Canada, and Canadian-owned firms like Magna International expanded production during the 1970s. American unions and local political leaders in American communities lamented the loss of manufacturing facilities such as the 1977 Youngstown Sheet and Tube closure in Ohio, but they tended to blame countries to the Global South and Asia for job losses, not Canada.

The 1973 OPEC embargo and the increase in energy prices that accompanied it impacted Canada, but those events also helped expand the country's energy sector. The western provinces, especially British Columbia and Alberta, attracted considerable internal migration as Canadian workers sought new job opportunities. The oil and gas industry was a central part of Canada's crucial natural resource sector, and that sector was still pivotal in the country's economy despite policymaking attention devoted to the manufacturing sector. Labor–management relations in the resource sector were at times contentious. Part of the oil and gas industry was unionized – such as the processing and distribution businesses – but the exploration and extraction sectors were non-union. Mining was overwhelmingly unionized, as exemplified by Inco in Sudbury, Ontario. The pulp and paper industry was also highly unionized. Fishing and fish processing was unionized. Farming was generally non-union, but food processing often was unionized.

Economic change in the mid-1970s brought a more hostile response toward labor from management, and public and private sector employers adopted different approaches to meeting the common objective of driving down wages. Corporate management pushed unions through collective bargaining, while governments used legislative means to control costs. For example, many unions had successfully negotiated Cost-of-Living Allowance (COLA) clauses into their collective agreements, and employers in the 1950s and 1960s were often willing to accept COLA since corporate profits were still relatively robust.[19]

A COLA clause links wages to increases in the Consumer Price Index (CPI) and does so separate from any percentage wage increases that a union negotiates with an employer. It would add money to a person's hourly rate of pay once CPI exceeded a level specified in a collective agreement. For instance, a union could negotiate a 3 percent wage increase every year in a three-year agreement. For someone making $8 per hour in 1970, that would have meant making $8.74 by 1973. However, if the CPI increased on average by 3.8 percent per year between 1970 and 1973 in Canada, and the collective agreement included COLA clauses that activated when the CPI exceeded 3 percent, then a much higher hourly rate would be paid. A person making $8 per hour in 1970 with a 3-percent wage increase thus would have actually been making $9.78 per hour by 1973 when COLA was added to negotiated increases.[20] Employers were consequently keen to take whatever steps were necessary to eliminate COLA clauses from collective agreements. There were several instances across Canada in the 1970s of employers either forcing strikes or actually locking-out workers in order to remove COLA clauses from collective agreements.[21]

Governments adopted a different approach, although there were public sector strikes when workers had the ability to strike. The federal government had power over wages and prices that exceeded any authority that a provincial or municipal government could wield. The Trudeau government responded to rising post-1973 inflation by imposing wage and price controls through an Anti-Inflation Board. Wage controls were placed on the increases that could be negotiated through collective bargaining, but not on the salaries paid to corporate managers and executives.[22] The Canadian labor movement responded to wage and price controls by mounting a national day of protest on

October 14, 1976, which was the closest that Canada has ever come to experiencing a national general strike.[23] The Canadian Labor Congress coordinated the protest effort, but the Trudeau government did not alter its policy course.

The formation of the first Parti Québécois (PQ) government in Quebéc in 1976 was another important moment for the Canadian labor movement, even though the party's sovereigntist political agenda was anathema to most anglophone Canadians. The PQ was a coalition of people on the left, urban professionals, some business leaders, and Québeckers who lived in overwhelmingly francophone regions of Québec. It was not popular with Québec's large indigenous Cree community. The PQ introduced pro-union labor legislation, including a ban on the use of replacement workers during a strike. That aspect of Québec labor law drew positive comments from union activists in English Canada, and it also helped ensure that Québec had a strong labor movement. The PQ was not a socialist party, but showed social democratic leanings in its policies and that aspect of its policy agenda was generally not recognized in English Canada due to a fixation on the party's sovereignty agenda.

Canadian Unions in the 1970s

Union density expanded in Canada during the 1970s, and the composition of the labor movement also evolved. Public sector unions such as the Canadian Union of Public Employees (CUPE) gradually became more central to the movement. Private sector unions were still often part of the Canadian regions of American-based organizations. There were indications in the 1970s that Canadian union leaders were increasingly chafing against the leadership style of their American international union offices. American unions did not adopt a concessionary bargaining approach during the decade – meaning willingness to give back gains that had previously been made – but they tolerated little internal dissent. This was most clearly evident in the internal actions of the International Brotherhood of Teamsters (IBT). The Teamsters were led through the 1960s by Jimmy Hoffa, who was a highly effective at making gains at the bargaining table but was also associated with organized crime. The Teamsters were a large union with over a million members in the 1970s, but they had difficulty losing associated with corruption and criminal activity. Hoffa was jailed for fraud and other crimes in 1967 and was attempting to regain leadership of the Teamsters after his release 1971, then disappeared under mysterious circumstances in 1975.[24]

The rise of public sector unions brought more women into the movement. Women encountered barriers entering employment in the public and private sectors and were usually paid less than men even when performing the same jobs. It was common in Canada into the 1970s for women to lose employment because of pregnancy. Sexual harassment was a significant problem in many workplaces. The entry of women into unionized jobs led to them also becoming activists and assuming leadership roles. Grace Hartman was elected president of CUPE in 1975 and was actually jailed for leading an illegal strike.[25]

Gender-based pay disparity led to women in unions pushing for pay equity. Pay equity means equal pay for work of equal value and is assessed based on skill, effort, responsibility, and working conditions. The push for pay equity began in the federal public service and then spread into the private sector, most notably with a case at Bell Canada. Management generally opposed pay equity due to the prospect of increased payroll cost. The labor movement was not initially united in the pursuit of pay equity – public sector unions began the push for it – and it would only be in later years that the labor movement more uniformly supported it.

The Canadian labor movement's ongoing association with the NDP continued to differentiate it from its American counterpart. An NDP government was elected in 1969 in Manitoba and was led by Ed Schreyer. Saskatchewan elected an NDP government led by Allan Blakeney in 1971. British Columbia elected its first NDP government in 1972. That government, led by Dave Barrett, only had one term but it passed an array of pro-labor legislation including making it easier for workers to organize unions.[26] The Barrett government quarreled with BC's business community as it also took control of several forestry operations – a key section of the province's economy – and turned them into crown corporations. The provincial NDP parties were not equally transformative, and the federal party did not rise above third place in parliament, but they were far more progressive on labor rights that Progressive Conservative or Liberal governments. The provincial and federal wings of the NDP benefited enormously from the support of labor activists and their unions in the 1970s.

Canadian Management in the 1970s

Canadian management in the 1970s functioned somewhat differently than its American counterpart. There was certainly recognition that management in the United States and Canada was different than Japanese management, as the latter involved practices such as Kaizen, but there were also subtle differences between Canadian and American management practices as it pertained to labor–management interaction. Labor relations in the public sector could be as contentious as anything experienced in the private sector, and Canada Post was a leading example of how confrontational labor–management interaction could become. Postal workers were represented by three unions in the 1970s: the Canadian Union of Postal Workers (CUPW), the International Brotherhood of Electrical Workers, and the Letter Carriers Union of Canada.

Postal workers considered Canada Post management to be heavy-handed, and there was considerable surveillance of workers. The labor–management environment was tense, and significant strikes occurred. The federal government used legislation – commonly called back-to-work – to force public sector workers off picket lines and back to their jobs. In 1979, CUPW president Jean-Claude Parrot was jailed for defying a back-to-work law. The use of that type of law was unique compared with what occurred in the United States. An American president has the power to intervene in a labor dispute under the auspices of the Taft–Hartley Act, but only if a federal judge can be convinced that a strike is impacting the national safety or health.[27]

The cumbersome nature of the American congressional legislative process would make it enormously difficult for the US Congress or a state legislature to even attempt to pass back-to-work legislation, and such legislation would immediately be challenged in court if it could be passed. Local and state law enforcement officers were sent to picket lines in the United States during the 1970s, even when there was no evidence that strikers were showing any signs of violence. The fact that most US public sector workers could not strike meant that governments showed little interest in using legislation to stop labor disputes. As Leo Panitch and Donald Swartz recount, Canadian federal and provincial governments showed little hesitation to use back-to-work laws against striking public sector workers as the post-war decades progressed.[28]

Private sector management was also more aggressive toward unions, and there were some particularly notable struggles. One such struggle occurred in the summer of 1978 when women at Fleck Industries in Centralia, Ontario went on strike. Fleck was an auto parts manufacturing firm named for owner James Fleck, and the workers were overwhelmingly female. Fleck resisted the strike and called upon the provincial government to send the Ontario Provincial Police (OPP) to ensure that the strikers did not become violent. There was no evidence that the striking workers were becoming violent but, at one point, there were more OPP officers in the Centralia area than there were women on the picket line.[29]

The rise of public sector unionization in the 1970s led Canadian management to view the public sector as separate but still an influence on private sector labor–management interaction. The extension of collective bargaining rights to the public sector was anathema to corporate Canada. For instance, the Canadian Association of Manufacturers generally opposed public sector unionization in correspondence to government officials, especially the prospect of public sector workers striking, of course without acknowledging the enormous power that government could exert over the employment relationship as both employer and legislator.[30]

Strikes and lockouts are specific moments in the timeline of labor–management interaction, and the actual labor relations process occurs through routine collective bargaining and ongoing struggles that happen in unionized workplaces. Those struggles are largely unknown to the wider public, but they are what ultimately shape the labor–management process. The methods that unions used to organize new workplaces and represent workers were much the same in the 1970s as they had been in the late 1940s. Major legislation often does not alter over time, and the main contents of labor laws like the Ontario Labor Relations Act did not change from the time that they were passed in the late 1940s up to the 1970s. Unions had to use those regulations to organize workers and then use the structures in place to interact with management.

Management in a unionized workplace is essentially able to run an organization in an unfettered manner unless there is a regulation, law, or clause in a collective agreement that stipulates otherwise. This meant that there was nothing to stop management from using new methods to manipulate relations with workers and their unions. For example, in 1960 Massachusetts Institute of Technology professor Douglas McGregor identified two types of management: Theory X and Theory Y. Theory X management was authoritarian and drew on a tradition going back to Frederick Winslow Taylor with the view that workers had to be monitored and made to work.[31]

Theory Y management was participatory and assumed that people wanted to work. Theory X management was really the only model used up to the 1970s, and it served to help unions organize as workers often wanted protection from tyrannical management. Personnel management was morphing into Human Resource Management in the 1970s and, along with managers being encouraged to be more Theory Y than X, the overall renewed effort from management was to convince workers that they did not need to unionize. Personality testing was also used to assess people in a range of activities, including education and employment. As Merve Emre recounted, the Myers–Briggs Type Indicator was a leading personality assessment and it helped management control workplaces.[32]

Canadian managers may not have learned much about workplace issues if they studied business and management at a university in the 1970s, but they could if they attended one of the country's still new community colleges and especially if they were sent to an internal corporate training course or seminar. Corporate training for managers often focused on how to deal with problem employees. For instance, Bell Canada, Labatt, and Eaton's all provided training on how to motivate employees and deal with those who were considered problematic. The overall message that managers received from corporate executives was that unions were something from the past, workers did not need them, and they should not be permitted in the public sector. Management was becoming more sophisticated in how it opposed unions, but unions were dependent on established tactics to mount a response.[33]

The 1980s

The 1970s marked the beginning of the end of the post-war labor–management system, and the 1980s were a decisive turning point for labor–management relations although the change was more acute in the United States than in Canada. Neo-conservative political ideology was ascendant beginning in the early years of the decade, global economic integration accelerated, and the Cold War remarkably came to a close. Those three events and trends influenced how workers and employers interacted with each other, and the latter group had ever more initiative in the labor–management process than the former possessed.

Neo-conservatism had been gestating through the post-war decades, but Canadian and American labor movements had been largely unaware of what was coming. Neo-conservative political, social, and economic thought was meant to be new conservatism but it was really extolling a return to pre-New Deal and even pre-Progressive Era policy. Unions knew about John Maynard Keynes and approved of economic policies that pursued objectives like full employment, but they had not heard of Friedrich von Hayek. Hayek was a contemporary of Keynes – the two of them were actually on friendly terms – but had diametrically opposing views on the role of the state in society. Whereas Keynes felt that an activist government was necessary to ensure social cohesion, Hayek believed that excessive state involvement in an economy led to tyranny and the loss of personal freedom. Both views were shaped by the experience of seeing Europe consumed by total war.

The Keynesian era persisted in Canada until 1984. The Trudeau government had shown an affinity for wage and price controls, but it was a government that was interested in having a role in Canada's economy. The Canadian government still held a significant portfolio of crown corporations in the early 1980s including Air Canada and Petro Canada. Trudeau stepped down in 1984 and was briefly replaced by John Turner. Turner was then soundly defeated later in 1984 by a Progressive Conservative party led by Brian Mulroney. Mulroney has been compared to Ronald Reagan and Britain's Margaret Thatcher, but he was more of a political opportunist than ideologue. He did believe in making Canada a more friendlier environment for business, and crucially brought Canada into a free trade agreement with the United States in 1988. Corporations in the United States and Canada became more powerful during the 1980s as a result of such policy changes.

American Unions in the 1980s

The American labor movement entered the 1980s essentially hoping that the new decade would not be worse than the previous one had been for unions. Ronald Reagan completed Richard Nixon's aspiration of drawing blue-collar Democrats to the Republican party, and indeed exceeded it as he also attracted suburban voters that previously voted Democrat. There were some unions, such as the Teamsters, that endorsed Republican candidates and that included endorsing Reagan in 1984. In 1980, Reagan was also endorsed by a federal public sector union called the Professional Air Traffic Controllers' Association (PATCO).[34] PATCO was a comparatively small union whose members had the important job of operating America's civilian air traffic control network. As Joseph McCartin has shown, interaction between PATCO and the US Federal Aviation Authority (FAA) was a textbook example of how poor labor–management relations could lead to collective bargaining disputes that had national implications.

PATCO went on strike in 1981 and, although later interpretations of the strike suggested that Reagan was determined to fire the strikers, he in fact was interested in seeing the FAA conclude a new collective agreement with the union. Reagan may have been mindful of his terms as president of the Screen Actors Guild from 1947 to 1952 and again from 1959 to 1960 when he thought about how to deal with the strike.[35] PATCO had forced previous Republican administrations to back down and, infuriated with FAA management, felt that Reagan would also back down. The union went on strike, and it was over barely after it started. Reagan, hearing the influence of right-wing advisors in the White House, fired all 10,000 controllers. They were replaced by military air traffic controllers. The PATCO strike was a major turning point in the history of American labor–management relations. The Reagan administration's response to the strike sent a signal to employers that breaking unions rather than negotiating with them was an acceptable labor–management practice. Strike activity declined even further during the 1980s as unions faced more aggressive management behavior.

There were instances of genuine national labor militancy in the 1980s, and one key example was the 1988 Writers' Guild of America strike. When members of the general public think of unions, there is an understandable reflex to view them in terms of public sector or industrial employment. In fact, the impact of unionized workers is seen every time someone sits in front of a television screen or in a movie theatre, and often when attending a rock concert or other live performance. Entertainment industry workers face a raft of conditions that spur them to unionize including precarity, wages, and control of their creative work. Residual payments for reruns of television programs were a key issue, and the 1988 strike resulted in somewhat of a compromise between television studios and writers as the studios won a sliding residual scale that they wanted while the writers made some financial gains. The strike lasted 150 days.[36]

Professional sports are another form of entertainment where viewers and fans may not expect to find unions, but all major professional sports leagues in both the United States and Canada are unionized. Being a professional athlete was often a part-time occupation into the early 1970s. There were some marquee players who earned high salaries and made money from commercial endorsements, but there were few who grew rich from their earnings. That trend changed as the 1970s progressed. For example, Bobby Orr was the first National Hockey League (NHL) player to receive a $1 million contract that paid out over five years in 1971. Major League Baseball (MLB) player compensation hit the million-dollar mark in the late 1970s, and National Football League (NFL) salaries did not begin to break the $1 million per year mark until the 1980s.[37]

Increases in professional athlete salaries were principally driven by higher professional sports profits and player demands to share those profits through collective bargaining. The most notable example of this trend was the MLB Players' Association's hiring of Marvin Miller from the United Steelworkers of America in 1966 to be executive director of the association. Miller negotiated agreements that gradually made players wealthier, and the MLB in turn shaped collective bargaining in other sports leagues. Labor–management relations in professional sports share a similarity with practices in the television and film industries as an additional party – agents – are involved in negotiations. Collective agreements in entertainment and professional sports provide salary minimums, health benefits, and retirement plans and player and performer agents are free to negotiate pay beyond minimum amounts.[38]

The 1980s were a decade of decline for American private sector unions, but public sector unionization stayed relatively stable despite the disastrous outcome of the PATCO strike. Some unions, particularly those in protective services, maintained high unionization rates and made significant bargaining gains. The movement was increasingly dominated by a handful of unions with large memberships including the National Education Association, American Federation of Teachers, the Teamsters, and the Service Employees International Union. The teachers' unions became highly influential in the movement due to their membership numbers.

American Management in the 1980s

There was little tolerance of worker dissent despite the outward impression given that corporations were inclusive environments. The new corporations that appeared in the 1980s were in industries such as electronics and information technology that were not known for unionization. Companies associated with Silicon Valley, like Apple, were in a state – California – with a relatively high rate of unionization by American standards but their workers did not form unions. Unionization among professional and technical workers outside of those employed in education tended to be low, with a range of factors impeding unionization, including professional workers having more affinity with professional identity than with being working class.

The 1980s PATCO strike was followed by a 1983 strike at Phelps Dodge that lasted for almost three years. The PATCO strike has becoming permanently associated with the Reagan years and greater management hostility toward unions, but the Phelps Dodge strike was of equal importance. In both cases, replacement workers were used by employers. The PATCO strikers were blacklisted and were only able to return to the FAA following the 1992 election of Bill Clinton, a Democrat, as president.[39] As Jonathan Rosenblum described, there was a significant level of state government involvement in the Phelps Dodge strike. The strike occurred in Arizona. Democratic governor Bruce Babbitt deployed the state National Guard in order to facilitate the movement of replacement workers into the Phelps Dodge copper mine. Replacement workers were eventually able to vote in favor of an employer settlement offer that striking unionized workers had rejected.[40]

American management benefited from considerable politicization of NLRB during the 1980s. The board was chaired by Donald Dotson for much of the Reagan years, and he led a Republican majority on the board that turned against labor rights and extended more power to employers.[41] The US Supreme Court was also moving to the right of the ideological spectrum by the early 1980s. A landmark 1980 decision called *NLRB vs. Yeshiva University* held that faculty members at private universities exercised managerial authority, which in turn precluded them from unionizing under the National Labor Relations Act.[42] In 1988, the court ruled in *Communication Workers of America vs Beck* that unions may only use membership dues money for activities relating to collective bargaining and not for political purposes.[43] Such Supreme Court decisions made it difficult for workers to unionize and also circumscribed their ability to represent their members, while further tilting the labor relations process toward management. The change in political environment, the type of corporations that emerged during the decade, and the gradual shift in legal environment all combined to enable management to be more hostile toward unions.

Canadian Unions in the 1980s

Canadian unions entered the 1980s angered by the ongoing impact of wage and price controls, and more successful in the political arena than their American counterparts. Union density in Canada remained relatively stable, although declines in the private sector were beginning to appear. Canada's service sector continued to grow in the 1980s, and much of it remained non-union. Public sector unions grew in importance, with the CUPE being the largest union in the country. Relations within the labor movement were at times fractious, and private sector and public sector unions did not often coalesce around a broad public policy program despite the best efforts of the Canadian Labor Congress (CLC) to achieve consensus.

The most significant development within the movement involved the shift away from links with industrial unions based in the United States, which involved a major break in the auto workers' union. Canadian members of the UAW were for years referred to as Region 7 of the union's organization before becoming the Canadian Region in the 1970s. The union was highly active politically and had a major media presence. Newspapers were still major news outlets in the 1980s, and many Canadian newspapers still had labor reporters on staff during those years. The UAW and other unions cultivated contacts in print and broadcast media.

The UAW's Canadian leadership was a vocal force against accepting bargaining concessions, and that stance ultimately led to the creation of a new union. The UAW international was led by Owen Bieber in the early 1980s and the Detroit automakers pushed for concessions in an effort to make themselves more competitive with their Japanese counterparts. Bieber was open to moving away from percentage hourly increases in every year of a collective agreement but Bob White, director of the Canadian region, was adamantly opposed to giving concessions. The situation came to a climax during a 1984 strike against GM in Canada. Bieber accepted an agreement with concessions for American UAW members and automatically expected that the same terms would be accepted in Canada. White led Canadian GM members on a brief strike that led to a distinct Canadian agreement that included guaranteed annual increases. The negotiations were also chronicled in a documentary called *The Final Offer*, which is most well-known film ever made about a strike in Canada. The UAW's American leadership was enraged that White adopted a different bargaining agenda, and the Canadian Auto Workers union (CAW) was formed in 1985.[44]

Not all Canadian regions of US-based international unions broke away to form independent labor organizations but a majority of union members in Canada belonged to Canadian-based unions by the end of the 1980s, whereas the reverse had been the case in the 1960s. The Canadian workers who stayed in American-based unions, like the USWA and the International Association of Machinists and Aerospace Workers, enjoyed more autonomy after their leaderships saw what happened to the UAW.

Canadian Management in the 1980s

There were instances of greater employer hostility toward labor shown by Canadian management in the 1980s, but it was not a scale seen in the United States. Canadian governments showed continued interest in using back-to-work legislation during the decade but did not do anything like firing all of the nation's air traffic controllers. The 1984 election of Brian Mulroney initially concerned the labor movement as the Progressive Conservative party was considered more hostile toward labor than the Liberals, although the Liberal Party of Canada was and continues to be an ideologically malleable entity that can go from issuing pro-union policy statements to quickly embracing wage and price legislation. Mulroney came into office promising "pink slips and running shoes" for the federal public service – meaning layoff notices and the means to walk out of government offices – but an assault on the federal public service never materialized to the extent that it did in the United States.[45]

The nature of labor law framework helped prevent disputes between unions and employers from having the same kind of national scope that was evident in the United States. A Canadian government could have of course tried to fire thousands of federal public sector workers, as was done to PATCO, but there was no need to do so because of the ability to use back-to-work legislation. A conflict on the scale of the Phelps Dodge strike could have happened in any Canadian province, and there were major conflicts in the different provinces, but the influence of such events did not necessarily have the same national impact as a dispute under national labor law in the United States.

For example, there was a bitter strike at Gainers' Meatpacking in Edmonton in 1986 that lasted six months. The company was owned by Peter Pocklington – also the owner of the NHL's Edmonton Oilers – and he sought to slash wages and eliminate the employee pension plan.[46] The strike received considerable national media attention and was a leading example of a reactionary business owner trying to break a union for no other reason than wanting to maximize profit. Other larger and more established companies also worked to prevent further unionization. For instance, another attempt to organize Eaton's department stores in the Toronto area was met with fierce management opposition. In the end, one store did unionize and Eaton's management responded by adjusting the firm's HR policies to ensure more active front-line management involvement in employee communication forums.[47]

High union density in the Canadian public service meant that union avoidance was not a viable strategy for public service management. Public sector managers instead used established collective bargaining methods to challenge unions, and unions did the same if they were unable to strike. Interest arbitration, which pertained to the actual content of collective agreements, was also found in the Canadian public sector to a greater extent than in the United States. The threat of back-to-work legislation was ever present for public sector workers, especially at the provincial and federal levels, as governments had shown considerable willingness to use legislatures to end public employee strikes. As seen in Table 3.1, union density rates in Canada and the United States diverged even further in the 1970s and 1980s.

Table 3.1 Union Density in Canada and the United States, 1970 and 1989

	1970	1989
Canada	33.6	36.2
United States	29.6	16.4

Source: Panitch and Swartz, 245.

Two Hard Decades

The 1970s and 1980s were challenging for unions in Canada and the United States, and the period brought mixed results for management. American business was clearly led to believe that attacking the socio-economic role of organized labor was acceptable. Canadian management adopted different approaches to labor–management relations depending on whether it was a public or private sector environment. Public sector unions became more central to the labor movements in both countries, while the Canadian and American economies began to become even more integrated following the passage of the 1988 Canada–US Free Trade Agreement. That agreement did not initially harm Canadian industrial workers to the extent feared by the labor movement's leadership, but it set the stage for attacks on labor rights in coming decades.

The 1980s ended with a remarkable event when the Berlin Wall fell in 1989 and the Cold War began to end. It seemed like a period of lasting peace and prosperity was assured in Canada and the United States. The end of Communism in Eastern Europe regrettably did not lead to economic peace as capitalism became even more ascendant than it had previously been, and greater economic integration and competition emerged. Labor–management interaction in Canada and the United States had been diverging since the late 1960s, and that divergence became more marked as union density was stable in Canada while it precipitously declined in the United States by the end of the 1980s. The political agendas in each country were also different as Canada continued to have a viable three-party system that featured a social democratic party, while the United States remained dominated by a two-party system that included one party – the Democrats – that increasingly showed itself as interested in talking with capital as with labor. The next two decades would bring greater divergence and more challenges.

Notes

1 Eric Loomis, *A History of America in Ten Strikes* (New York: New Press, 2018), 168–174.
2 Philip F. Rubio, *Undelivered: From the Great Postal Strike of 1970 to the Manufactured Crisis of the U.S. Postal Service* (Chapel Hill: University of North Carolina Press, 2020), 1–3.
3 Jefferson Cowie, *Stayin' Alive: The 1970s and the Last Days of the Working Class* (New York: The New Press, 2010), 2.
4 Cowie, *Stayining Alive*, 128.
5 Ibid., 139.
6 Ibid., 275.
7 Lane Windham, *Knocking on Labor's Door: Union Organizing in the 1970s and the Roots of a New Economic Divide* (Chapel Hill: University of North Carolina Press, 2017), 3.
8 Windham, *Knocking on Labor's Door,* 4–6.
9 Ibid., 85.
10 On the development and impact of the 1978 Civil Service Reform Act see Charles J. Coleman, "The Civil Service Reform Act of 1978: Its Meaning and Roots," *Labor Law Journal* (April, 1980), pp. 200–209.
11 Mel Van Elteren, *Managerial Control of American Workers: Methods and Technology from the 1880s to Today* (Jefferson, North Carolina: McFarland and Company, 2017), 100.
12 Van Elteren, *Managerial Control of American Workers,* 100–101.
13 See Martin Levitt, *Confessions of a Union Buster* (New York: Crown Publishers, 1993).
14 Loomis, *A History of America in Ten Strikes,* 164.
15 Shannon Clark, *The Making of the American Creative Class: New York's Cultural Workers and Twentieth-Century Consumer Capitalism* (New York: Oxford University Press, 2021) includes discussion of white-collar unions in World War II and the years immediately following the war.
16 William Adler, *Mollie's Job: A Story of Life and Work on the Global Assembly Line* (New York: Scribner, 2000).
17 Jefferson Cowie, *Capital Moves: RCA's Seventy-Year Quest for Cheap Labor* (Ithaca: Cornell University Press, 1999).
18 Volkswagen, "#TBT – The Rich History of Volkswagen's Puebla Plant," 16 July 2020, https://media.vw.com/en-us/releases/1354.
19 Not all unions pursued COLA clauses, but most sought them. The Oil, Chemical, and Atomic Workers Union (OCAW), one of the forerunners of the Energy and Chemical Workers Union (ECWU) did not pursue COLA clauses. On this policy toward COLA, and other aspects of energy and chemical industry bargaining in Canada, see Wayne Roberts, *Cracking the Canadian Formula: The Making of the Energy and Chemical Workers Union* (Toronto: Between the Lines Books, 1990), 128–129.
20 Data is based on Bank of Canada, "Inflation Calculator," 30 April 2022, www.bankofcanada.ca/rates/related/inflation-calculator/.

21 Jason Russell, *Our Union: UAW/CAW Local 27 from 1950 to 1990* (Edmonton: Athabasca University Press, 2011), 117–122.

22 Craig Heron and Charles Smith, *The Canadian Labour Movement: A Short History*, third edition (Toronto: Lorimer, 2020), 109.

23 Heron and Smith, *The Canadian Labour Movement,* 110.

24 On the life of Jimmy Hoffa see Thaddeus Russell, *Out of the Jungle: Jimmy Hoffa and the Remaking of the American Working Class* (New York: A.A. Knopf, 2001).

25 *Grace Hartman: The First Woman to Lead a Major Canadian Union*, directed by Todd Harris (Toronto: Labour Video Communications, 1997).

26 Andrew Jackson, "BC Premier Dave Barrett Showed the Canadian Left How to Make Change Happen," *Jacobin*, 20 July 2021, www.jacobinmag.com/2021/07/british-columbia-dave-barrett-ndp-social-credit.

27 Jean-Claude Parrot, *My Union, My Life: Jean-Claude Parrot and the Canadian Union of Postal Workers* (Halifax: Fernwood, 2005), 115–134.

28 Leo Panitch and Donald Swartz, *From Consent to Coercion: The Assault on Trade Union Freedoms, third edition* (Aurora: Garamond, 2003), 247–252.

29 Heron and Smith, *The Canadian Labour Movement*, 144.

30 Archives of Ontario, Canadian Manufacturers' Association Fonds, RG7-1-0-1881.1, Box B353713, W.H. Whiteman, CMA, to Ontario Minister of Labour Bette Stephenson, 16 September 1976.

31 Van Elteren, *Managerial Control of American Workers*, 99.

32 Merve Emre, *The Personality Brokers: The Strange History of Myers-Briggs and the Birth of Personality Testing* (New York: Doubleday, 2018), 159–176.

33 See Jason Russell, *Making Managers in Canada, 1945–1995: Companies, Community Colleges, and Universities* (New York: Routledge, 2020), 35–67.

34 Gerald R. Boyd, "Teamsters Vote to Endorse Reagan," *New York Times*, 31 August 1984, Section A, Page 12.

35 Screen Actors Guild – American Federation of Television and Radio Artists (SAG-AFTRA), "SAG Presidents," 30 April 2022, www.sagaftra.org/about/our-history/sag-presidents

36 Los Angeles. Times Archives, "Writers Strike Chronology," *Los Angeles Times,* 4 August 1988, www.latimes.com/archives/la-xpm-1988-08-04-mn-10237-story.html.

37 Kevin Griffin, "This Week in History: Bobby Orr Becomes First NHL 'Millionaire,'" *Vancouver Sun*, 25 August 2017, https://vancouversun.com/news/local-news/this-week-in-history-bobby-orr-becomes-first-nhl-millionaire.

38 On collective bargaining in Major League baseball see Marvin Miller, *A Whole Different Ballgame: The Sport and Business of Baseball* (Secaucus: Carol Publishing Group, 1991).

39 Joseph A. McCartin, *Collision Course: Ronald Reagan, the Air Traffic Controllers, and the Strike that Changed America* (New York: Oxford University Press, 2011), 356–357.

40 Jonathan D. Rosenblum, *Copper Crucible: How the Arizona Miners' Strike of 1983 Recast Labor-Management Relations in America* (Ithaca: Cornell ILR Press, 1995), 107–115.

41 Timothy J. Minchin, *Labor Under Fire: A History of the AFL-CIO since 1979* (Chapel Hill: University of North Carolina Press, 2017), 113.

42 *National Labor Relations Board v. Yeshiva University*, 444 U.S. 672 (1980).

43 *Communications Workers of America v. Beck*, 487 U.S. 735 (1988).

44 Bob White, *Hard Bargains: My Life on the Line* (Toronto: McClelland and Stewart, 1987), 302–335.

45 Jason Russell, *Leading Progress: The Professional Institute of the Public Service of Canada, 1920–2020.* (Toronto: Between the Lines, 2020), 80.

46 James Wilt, "Remembering the Gainers Strike," 6 March 2016, https://www.rankandfile.ca/remembering-the-gainers-strike/.

47 Russell, *Making Mangers in Canada*, 50.

4 The 1990s and 2000s

The 1990s and 2000s brought enormous change in Canada and the United States, including in relations between labor and management. Technology further altered the nature of work as the Internet grew from something that was used by a comparatively small number of people to an integral part of everyday life. The Internet created new jobs, but other technologies eliminated or diminished other forms of work. Public policy become more oriented toward business interests as the impact of the fall of Communism in Eastern Europe became fully evident. Neo-liberal economic thought became an even greater part of economic policy in the United States and Canada than it had in the 1980s. Management, public and private, became more hostile toward labor but unions also pushed back against management hostility. There were periods of major economic growth, but also grievous turmoil.

The United States in the 1990s

The US entered the final decade of the twentieth century by fighting a short, sharp, and victorious war against Iraq. The collapse of the Soviet Bloc led newly democratic Eastern European countries to actively seek economic integration into the European Union and membership in the North Atlantic Treaty Organization. An attempted 1991 coup in Russia led to the end of the Soviet Union, and democracy and capitalism appeared to have won a lasting triumph over communism and socialism. The fact that China, the most populous country in the world, had a Communist government was largely rationalized by the fact that it was actively embracing state capitalism. The 1990s were the decade when American economic, military, and political power reached its historical apogee. The United States was the world's sole superpower, its popular culture had spread around the world, and it dominated the global economy.

DOI: 10.4324/9780429294938-5

The US was led by Democratic president Bill Clinton for all but two years of the 1990s. Republican George H.W. Bush had handily defeated Democratic nominee Michael Dukakis in the 1988 election and, as Ronald Reagan's vice-president, he seemed poised to continue Republican control of the White House into the 1990s. Bush led the victorious Desert Storm coalition, and the US economy was strong as the 1980s ended. The economic and political situation changed in 1991 with a short but significant recession that led to double-digit unemployment. That recession was also the first one to lead to significant layoffs among managerial employees across the country. Clinton, a relatively unknown Democratic governor from Arkansas, won his party's nomination in 1992. The Democrats retook the White House and maintained control of Congress, including maintaining over three decades as the majority party in the House of Representatives.

Labor activists had high hopes for Bill Clinton, especially after eight years of the Reagan administration and four years of George H.W. Bush. Clinton brought progressive policymakers with him to Washington, including economist and future Secretary of Labor Robert Reich. Little actual progress was made by the Clinton administration when it came to improving the labor and employment law framework, mainly because the Democrats lost control of Congress in the 1994 mid-term elections and the Republicans maintained control until the end of Bill Clinton's term in office. The Clinton administration had aspirations for reforming the labor and employment law framework that went unrealized because of the 1994 electoral disaster. Clinton created the Commission on the Future of Worker–Management Relations in 1993 in response to the *Electromation, Inc. v. National Labor Relations Board* decision on company unions. It was more commonly called the Dunlop Commission, as it was chaired by noted labor arbitrator John T. Dunlop. The commission was an ambitious attempt to gather together interest groups and experts from across the labor–management spectrum to submit ideas on how to reform labor and employment law, and otherwise modernize the regulatory framework governing workplace relations.[1]

Management representatives who appeared before the Dunlop commission generally opposed changes to the existing labor–management legal framework, while unions and many academics supported change. The Railway Labor Relations act was one of the few areas of agreement between union and management representatives, as employers and unions regulated by it both indicated that they did not want to see it altered even though working conditions had changed in the airline and rail industries. The labor relations legal framework in the United States may well have incorporated at least some of the commission's recommendations had the Democrats been able to retain control of Congress during the Clinton years.[2]

The continued deterioration of labor–management interaction in the United States in the 1990s was often overshadowed by the decade's economic growth. The United States, Canada, and Mexico concluded the North American Free Trade Agreement (NAFTA) in 1993. 1992 US Reform Party candidate Ross Perot declared that Americans would hear a loud sucking sound as jobs went to Mexico after NAFTA was implemented and, his other policy positions aside, he was correct that NAFTA did lead to the movement of jobs from Canada and the United States to Mexico. Trade liberalization became a priority for western governments. The World Trade Organization (WTO) was created in 1995 as part of an agreement based on the long Uruguay Round of negotiations that focused on the General Agreement on Trade and Tariffs (GATT). GATT was designed to lower trade barriers, and the WTO was devised to enforce trade rules and adjudicate trade disputes between governments.[3]

The United States sat at the center of trade liberalization initiatives that were devised during the 1990s. The principal problem with such trade policy was that it was profoundly undemocratic. WTO dispute rulings were binding on countries that were signatories to GATT, and it was not possible for elected national representatives to ignore WTO decisions. Small- and medium-sized countries were particularly disadvantaged by the WTO. The United States lost disputes before the WTO but, as the world's leading economy and only real military superpower, it routinely ignored WTO decisions that it does not like. As Thomas Piketty has showed, income inequality had begun to widen in the 1980s and it became worse in the 1990s. Public unrest about income and wealth disparity did not become widespread until the latter years of the decade. The 1990s were a transition decade as the Cold War ended, the role of technology in everyday life changed, and globalization became seemingly unstoppable. It was a decade in which corporations became more powerful and workers and their unions struggled to respond to the changes facing them.[4]

American Unions in the 1990s

The American labor movement entered the 1990s with the United Auto Workers (UAW), one of its key unions, soon engaged in another strike that was as significant as PATCO's if not as well-publicized in the popular press. Caterpillar corporation is a manufacturer of heavy construction machinery such as excavators and bulldozers. It had a large, unionized workforce at the start of the 1990s and those workers were represented by the UAW. Caterpillar sold equipment around the world and was the world's leading heavy construction equipment manufacturer by the end of the 1970s. Caterpillar management was interested in cementing its hold on the construction machinery sector and decided that taking on the UAW was part of that strategy.[5]

The construction machinery industry went through a period of reduced activity in the early 1990s, which in turn impacted Caterpillar. The company's workforce declined from 90,000 in 1979 to 56,000 in 1991, with its UAW membership dropping from 40,500 to 15,100 in the same period. The company implemented new manufacturing technology and management methods that led to workforce reductions. Corporate leadership also changed its approach to labor–management relations.[6]

In 1991, Caterpillar management demanded an end to pattern bargaining, a two-tier wage system that would pay new workers less than those already employed by the company, and flexible work schedules. UAW members went on strike in November 1991, and then workers at plants who did not strike were locked out in February 1992. The labor action drew support from 22,000 UAW members. That strike ended in April 1992 when the union called an end to it on the face of management threats to bring in replacement workers.[7]

Another strike occurred at Caterpillar plants in 1994 and lasted for 17 months. The UAW again backed down when confronted with the threat of permanent job loss. Management had prepared for the second confrontation by training front-line managers and other non-union staff to perform unionized work, and also sent more work to non-unionized plants in the South in addition to importing components from overseas. The UAW filed complaints with the NLRB over management's conduct, but the end result was that an agreement was reached in 1998 that gave Caterpillar everything that it wanted including a two-tier wage structure and flexible work scheduling. The renewed collective bargaining agreement was six-years in duration, which is exceptionally long for an agreement in manufacturing.[8]

The dispute between the UAW and Caterpillar from 1991 to 1998 in many ways represents the challenges facing American unions during those years. Caterpillar took advantage of globalization and the ever-present non-union South to drive down wages in unionized factories, and the autoworkers' union proved unable to resist what occurred. There are differing views over whether or not the union suffered a major defeat, but the inescapable fact is that Caterpillar achieved much of what it wanted. That long dispute also signaled to major companies that taking a hard line in negotiations could bring success. It is also important to note that American unions benefited during most of the 1990s from an NLRB that had a Democratic majority appointed by Bill Clinton, but even that was not enough to compensate for overt management hostility.

Labor's disputes with employers did not always lead to major defeats like the one suffered at Caterpillar. The Teamsters' union went under federal government oversight in 1988 as a result of rampant corruption within that union, and it remained so until 2015.[9] Jimmy Hoffa was replaced by a succession of international presidents who were uninterested in democratic reform. The US government forced the Teamsters to permit direct election of national officers, and Ron Carey was elected as the union's president in 1992 under the new election procedures. He faced internal opposition from groups within the union that were associated with previous presidents such as Hoffa, and he also showed the willingness to challenge large corporations in a way that the union had not done in many years. Carey actually defeated Hoffa's son, James Hoffa, Jr., to be re-elected in 1996.[10]

By 1990s, the service sector expanded to include a wide range of companies that performed an equally broad range of functions, and courier companies were a major part of that sector. United Parcel Service (UPS) was the world's largest parcel delivery company in the mid-1990s, and its members were represented by the Teamsters. UPS management was interested in making greater use of part-time and casual labor and its full-time, unionized workers were well-compensated and earned wages that made it possible to pursue a middle-class lifestyle. Carey led 200,000 union members at UPS on a two-week strike in August, 1997 that led to the union gaining wage increases and enhancing job security. The strike was considered a success for the Teamsters and the wider American labor movement.[11]

The strike at UPS was a success, but American private sector unions faced conflicts that were more like what occurred at Caterpillar. Overall union membership remained constant at around 16 million members throughout the 1990s, but union density continued to edge downward as the non-unionized workforce grew. There were some areas where labor maintained considerable strength such as in the public service, transportation, and construction. Jobs in those areas could not be readily moved to another country. American manufacturing jobs continued to decline, and the new manufacturing jobs that were created were often located in states in the South. The situation would have likely been worse for American unions had a Democratic administration not been in office from 1992 to 2000, even though Bill Clinton did sign NAFTA into law and unions opposed free trade.

Average American citizens were receptive to unions, but much of the media messaging about organized labor was negative. The 1994 to 1995 Major League Baseball (MLB) strike had an especially negative impact on how people viewed unions. The strike happened because MLB owners wanted to impose a salary cap on players. The players pushed back, and the end result was the cancellation of the 1994 World Series. On a basic level, it was a dispute over limits being placed on player earnings, but it looked to the public like millionaires having a disagreement with billionaires at the expense of everyday sports fans.[12]

American Management in the 1990s

American management continued to evolve during the 1990s. Few corporate leaders spoke against globalization, and instead used it as a pretext for reorganizing their companies and sending work and production facilities to other countries. There was renewed interest in outsourcing work as established corporations sought to focus on what they regarded as core functions. The rise of the Internet and greater office computerization demonstrated to managers that they could employ more sophisticated methods to monitor and control workers.

Management theory altered again during the 1990s, with Total Quality Management (TQM) becoming popular among corporate consultants and senior executives. TQM is based on the work of W. Edwards Deming, an American whose theories on management gained little traction in the United States in the 1950s and 1960s but were widely embraced in Japan.[13] Deming can be regarded as a successor to Drucker, even though there were contemporaries, as TQM became more fashionable among managers than Management by Objectives.

TQM was ostensibly about eliminating production problems in order to enhance product and process quality. Attempts were also made to adapt it for use in the service industry. As Van Elteren described, TQM was a kind of synthesis of a variety of quality management ideas and the term Total Quality Management was actually coined by a US Navy psychologist named Nancy Warren. The challenge for workers was that, even though TQM was presented as something new, it was rooted in Taylorist methods of measuring and controlling work. It, therefore, was also an effort to control workers.[14]

The greater use of technology and related management methods to control the workplace posed new challenges for unions. For example, management began using Global Positioning System technology – another technology that started in the military – to track and discipline workers. Drug testing was another area of workplace surveillance, and it was not unusual in the United States by the 1990s for workers to be required to submit a urine sample as a condition of employment. Virtually all American states were still under the fire-at-will doctrine, meaning a person could be terminated without warning or cause, which further reinforced managerial control over workers.

Human Resource Management (HRM) was a growing academic subject at post-secondary institutions across the United States – largely because it was one area of business that seemed to align reasonably well with other social science and humanities subjects – but the role of HRM in actually running organizations was uneven. A professional association called the Society for Human Resource Management (SHRM) was founded in 1948 to advance the training and stature of people working in the personnel function, and the SHRM professional designation became a popular learning option for people working in HR, and for graduates with Social Science and Humanities degrees who wanted to work in business. The HR function still continued to be a staff rather than line function into the end of the twentieth century, and consequently did not have the same influence as areas like marketing and finance.[15]

Canadian Unions in the 1990s

The Canadian labor movement entered the 1990s concerned about the impact of free trade, but not suffering from major internal divisions. That latter condition changed by the middle of the decade. Canada in the early 1990s had NDP governments in British Columbia, Saskatchewan, and Ontario. Having NDP governments in power in British Columbia and Saskatchewan annoyed Canada's business community, but it was hardly a novel situation since those provinces had previously experienced the NDP in power. The election of Bob Rae's NDP government in Ontario seemingly caught everyone in the province by surprise, including Rae.[16]

The Ontario business community, including the financial industry based on Toronto's Bay Street, was both enraged and appalled over the election of the Rae government. Rae expanded provincial spending, passed Employment Equity legislation to advance workers from equity-seeking groups, made it easier for unions to organize, and introduced a ban on the use of replacement workers during strikes and lockouts. Other legislation was passed, but those were some of the areas that most pertained to unions. The Ontario NDP was aligned with the provincial labor movement, and unions expected to see progressive policies introduced by Rae.

The Rae government had basically one year of reasonable popularity then began to feel the impact of the 1991 recession, which in turn put it into conflict with its labor allies. The government faced huge increases in deficit spending and responded by engaging in negotiations with public sector unions over what it called the Social Contract. The government reasoned that public sector payrolls and benefits were a huge part of overall budget costs, and that getting unions to agree to open collective agreements in order to attempt to improve the Ontario budget was good public policy.

Ontario's public sector unions were united in their opposition to the Social Contract. There have been a range of accounts of what transpired during the negotiations over public sector wage reductions, including by former CUPE Ontario president Sid Ryan. The furious reaction of public sector unions to the Social Contract, the terms of which were eventually imposed by the government, was exacerbated by the support that some private sector unions expressed for the government's public sector wage policies. This led to a rift in the Ontario and wider Canadian labor movements that still partially shapes labor's involvement with electoral politics into the twenty-first century.[17]

The Rae government was enormously unpopular by 1995, when it lost an election and was replaced by a newly resurgent Progressive Conservative party led by Mike Harris. Harris ran on a platform or repealing many of the measures introduced by Rae, including Employment Equity and the anti-replacement worker law. In fact, Harris went farther than what was described in his party's platform and changed the content of the Ontario Labor Relations Act to include references to the need for parties engaged in collective bargaining to recognize the need for change, and the need to promote productivity and flexibility in the workplace. Harris also significantly reduced welfare payments and was almost immediately engaged in confrontation with the province's public sector unions. The Ontario labor movement responded with Days of Action that involved huge demonstrations in major cities between 1995 and 1998.[18]

Canadian unions were also confronted with anti-labor policy, notably in Alberta, and also at the federal level. Alberta was long governed by its own Progressive Conservative party, and it was led by Ralph Klein for much of the 1990s. Klein, like Harris, was a populist who espoused neo-conservative political ideology. The Alberta government was flush with money in the 1990s, but Klein still fought with the province's public sector workers. The Klein government also formally studied the idea of introducing a Right-to-Work law in Alberta but decided against doing so as it would have had no economic benefit.[19]

The federal Liberal government led by Jean Chrétien governed Canada from 1993 to 2003, and he was subsequently replaced by Paul Martin as Liberal leader and prime minister. Chrétien was not overtly anti-union, although his government did pass back-to-work legislation to end a 1997 strike at Canada Post. The Chrétien government was faced with a major spending deficit and expanding overall national debt, the value of the Canadian dollar had dropped in comparison to the US dollar, and the business community argued that drastic spending cuts had to be made in order to improve the nation's finances.[20]

The government responded with a program of spending austerity, including the elimination of many jobs in the federal public service. There was further privatization of public services, such as turning the air traffic control system into a non-profit corporation called Nav Canada in 1996. The government's cost-cutting measures did eventually lead to balanced federal budgets, but at the cost of federal public sector jobs. Chrétien was not reviled by the Canadian labor movement like Harris and Klein were, and he did not attempt to alter the intent of federal public sector labor and employment legislation or pass overtly anti-union legislation such as Right-to-Work. There was nonetheless an overall pattern of imposing austerity on the Canadian federal public sector in the 1990s.

The legal framework regulating labor–management interaction in Canada did not experience a significant turn to the right during the 1990s, and decisions began to come from the Supreme Court of Canada that framed labor rights within the context of the Charter of Rights and Freedoms. The 1982 Constitution Act gave Canadians full control over constitutional matters, and it also included the Charter. A 1991 case – *Lavigne v. Ontario Public Service Employees Union* (OPSEU) – illustrated the role that the Charter could have on Canadian unions. Francis Mervyn Lavigne was an instructor at a community college called the Haileybury School of Mines, and he objected to having a portion of his union dues used for political purposes by OPSEU. His case was funded with assistance from a conservative lobbying group called the National Citizens' Coalition, which was for a time led by future Conservative Prime Minister Stephen Harper. The case eventually went to the Supreme Court of Canada, where not only did the justices uphold the right of OPSEU to use membership dues as the union chose, but also upheld the overall constitutionality of union members being required to pay dues or an equal amount to the union representing them in the workplace. The court affirmed the constitutionality of the Rand Formula.[21]

All Canadian unions cheered the *Lavigne* decision, and it represented a major point of divergence with the United States. The US Supreme Court had upheld mandatory dues payment for public sector workers in the 1977 *Abood v. Detroit Board of Education* case but the ongoing impact of Section 14B of the Taft–Hartley Act was still felt by American unions. The Supreme Court of Canada affirmed the legality of requiring union members to pay dues but, as subsequent analysis will show, the US Supreme Court eventually adopted a markedly different view of the matter.

Canadian private sector union membership declined in the 1990s, largely because of the closure of manufacturing facilities and difficult organizing in the service sector. Unions in manufacturing, especially the Canadian Auto Workers (CAW), were prominent voices in the labor movement but public sector unions increasingly represented unionized Canadians. There were other sectors where unions remained strong, such as construction and resource extraction and processing, but organizing workers in professional occupations was difficult. There was also the growing prevalence of precarious work in Canada, much as there was in the United States, and existing labor laws were ill-suited to organizing people employed on temporary and contract bases.

Canadian Management in the 1990s

Canada's public and private sector employers experienced major changes in the 1990s, but they were not under the kind of attacks that unions faced. The business community approved of the passage of the 1993 NAFTA agreement, liked the Liberal government's austerity program, and also supported the policies implemented by Harris and Klein. The main threat that part of the business community faced came from abroad, as corporations confronted greater international competition in many economic sectors. There were limits to how much competition corporate Canada would accept and industries like telecommunications, banking, and transportation were well protected by federal laws.

For instance, Canada's banking sector is dominated by six large Schedule One banks. A Schedule One bank is domestically owned, and its shares are widely held. Four of Canada's major banks – Bank of Montréal (BMO), Canadian Imperial Bank of Commerce (CIBC), Toronto Dominion (TD), and Royal Bank – proposed mergers to the federal government during the 1990s, but the mergers (CIBC and TD, BMO and Royal Bank) were rejected due to concerns about competition and concentration in the financial services industry. TD eventually merged with trust company Canada Trust, and that combined entity became one of the two largest banks in Canada. The financial services industry, including Canada's influential insurance companies, remained overwhelmingly non-union.

Canada's airline industry is also highly regulated and foreign carriers cannot operate in the domestic air travel market. It is also very difficult for a new carrier to enter the market. WestJet, a Calgary-based carrier, began flying in 1994 and remained non-union throughout the decade. Its cabin crews and pilots eventually unionized. Canada's telecommunications sector was also dominated by a small number of large firms, such as Rogers and Bell, and that the industry was also protected from foreign takeovers. The major telecommunications firms were also unionized, although jobs at companies like Rogers and Bell were highly vulnerable to technological change and outsourcing.

Canadian manufacturing continued to feature subsidiaries of major American companies, such the Detroit automakers and Japanese firms Honda and Toyota. Those two companies were careful to pay wages and benefits that were close to the compensation earned by members of the UAW and CAW, which made unionization difficult despite repeated efforts by unions in both countries to organize foreign transplant factories. Japanese management technique, as exemplified by the Kaizen method, also proved anathema to unionized workers. Most notably, Suzuki and General Motors (GM) operated a joint venture called CAMI automotive in Ingersoll, Ontario, that was supposed to new model for industrial relations in Canada. The plant was not open for very long before the workers – members of the CAW – were on strike. CAMI eventually became the sole property of GM.[22]

There were major Canadian manufacturing firms such as auto parts giant Magna International and transportation firm Bombardier but there was often a threat of successful Canadian manufacturing firms being taken over by foreign companies, often from the United States. Magna posed a particularly vexing challenge for unions because it used a culture of workplace paternalism as a union avoidance method. Federal governments went to great lengths to protect the finance, telecommunications, and air transportation industries from foreign involvement but did comparatively little to prevent other Canadian companies from being subsumed into the operations of global parent firms.

The collective voice of Canadian business became much more prominent in public discourse during the 1990s, with groups like the Canadian Chamber of Commerce and the Business Council on National Issues producing policy papers and sending representatives to appear in broadcast and print media to promote a pro-business agenda. That agenda included trumpeting free trade, deregulation, and privatization. Management felt quite emboldened as a corporate public policy agenda appeared to be ascendant. The fact that governments were actively challenging public employees throughout the decade further encouraged private sector employers to take a harder stance during their rounds of collective bargaining.

The 1990s ended with an event that showed labor's willingness to push back again neo-liberalism and what seemed like a relentless corporate agenda. Representatives of the WTO met in Seattle, Washington in 1999 and representatives from labor and social advocacy groups from across the United States, Canada, and beyond converged on the city to protest the WTO and the neo-liberal agenda that appeared to dominate the global economy. The WTO representatives were shocked at the scale of the protests, and the global media were transfixed by what was called the Battle of Seattle. It was a notable closure to the decade, and indeed to the twentieth century, as organized labor showed that it still had the power and resources to challenge corporate power.

The 2000s

The arrival of the twenty-first century was met with both hope and trepidation. A closely contested election resulted in Republican candidate George W. Bush winning the American presidency. His election was followed a year later by the catastrophic terrorist attacks that happened in New York City and Washington, DC on September 11, 2001. A third attack would have happened had the passengers on another plan not overpowered the hijackers on board, although that flight ultimately crashed in Pennsylvania. The minutiae of labor–management interaction are rarely mentioned in popular media and are instead parsed in narrower forums that are meant for practitioners and academics working in labor–management relations and human resources. The changes that the second Bush administration worked to implement to the labor–management framework were consequently not prominently featured in popular media. 9/11, the wars in Afghanistan and Iraq, Hurricane Katrina, and the 2008 global economic crisis instead dominated popular discourse in the 2000s.

The Bush administration benefited from Republican control of both houses of Congress from 2002 to 2006. The NLRB members appointed by Bush reversed previous rulings on issues such as the ability of graduate students to form unions. The US Supreme Court expanded the definition of supervisor, and thus limited who could potentially unionize, in the 2001 *Kentucky River* decision.[23] Labor law experts where extremely concerned that a vast array of workers, including trades people supervising apprentices, could be excluded from unionization because of the new definition of manager. In 2004, the Bush administration produced an economic report which mused that fast food work was actually a type of manufacturing.[24] This reclassification did not ultimately proceed, although adopting it would have immediately added scores of manufacturing jobs to official employment statistics.

The political and economic environment in Canada altered during the 2000s. The Liberal Party of Canada had benefited tremendously from facing a political right that was divided between the remains of the Progressive Conservative Party and the Reform Party. A series of electoral defeats led to a rapprochement between the two right-wing parties, and a united Conservative Party led by Stephen Harper was able to form a minority government in 2006. The Harper government proved to be driven by hard-right political ideology.

The 2008 financial crisis – the worst downturn since the Great Depression – compelled the Harper government to implement emergency spending measures to steady the Canadian economy, but unemployment still soared to levels not experienced in many years. As with the United States, changes that the government sought to make with regard to federal labor and employment law received insufficient coverage in the media. Canadian union leaders suspected that Harper was interested in introducing Right-to-Work at the federal level, but it was also possible that such a law would lead to labor mounting a legal challenge under the Charter of Rights and Freedoms. Harper did impose burdensome regulations on unions that were equivalent to Landrum–Griffin requirements in the United States in Bill C-377, although the Liberal government elected in 2015 repealed those regulations.

The political environment at the provincial level was occasionally similar to what happened federally, while different at other times. British Columbia was governed by a party that was officially called Liberal during the 2000s, but it was actually a conservative party. Alberta, Saskatchewan, and Manitoba had right-wing governments during the decade. Ontario voters replaced their right-wing government in 2003 with a Liberal one led by Dalton McGuinty, and in the process maintained a pattern of electing one party to form a national government and a different party provincially. Québec had a Liberal government for most of the 2000s. Prince Edward Island, New Brunswick, Nova Scotia, and Newfoundland and Labrador respectively elected Conservative, Liberal, and New Democratic governments. As with the United States and every other country around the world, the 2008 financial crisis was the greatest public policy challenge for governments at all levels in Canada.

American Unions in the 2000s

American unions faced major headwinds during the 2000s. The decade began with another important labor action, when the International Longshore and Warehouse Union went on strike at ports on the West Coast. Consumers benefited from a vast array of goods and services, and much of what was available on store shelves was imported from Asia. This fact meant that there was a continual flow of goods into ports at Los Angeles and Long Beach, and even a brief interruption in global supply chains drew and immediate and furious response from the business community. For a union, being able to bring a halt to imports of billions of dollars worth of goods through ports brought huge bargaining leverage. The strike showed the susceptibility of global supply chains to labor action. The Bush administration responded to the 2002 West Coast port strike by invoking the Taft–Hartley Act, which impacted over 10,000 workers at 29 ports. Bush was the first president since Nixon to invoke the act to end a strike.[25]

As Timothy Minchin described, the Bush years were difficult for the labor movement. Bush knew that the AFL–CIO opposed his candidacy, and he never met with federation representatives during his time in office. Nonetheless, a curious aspect of the American labor movement's power persisted. If someone who was politically astute and were to have come from another country and visited Washington, DC without knowing anything about the wider challenges facing American unions, they would have concluded that organized labor was powerful. As Minchin notes, AFL–CIO president John Sweeney was viewed as having maintained labor's political power despite the problem of membership declines. Labor's political influence was even recognized by the US Chamber of Commerce, and the AFL–CIO played a key role in the Democrats retaking control of Congress in 2006.[26]

The ongoing political influence of the AFL–CIO in Washington masked the problem that unions faced huge challenges with opposing government and business policies that were part of globalization. The UAW went from 1.5 million members in 1979 to 500,000 by 2009.[27] The United States lost 2.5 million manufacturing jobs in the 2000s.[28] More manufacturing work was moved to other countries because of lower business operating costs. Union leaders continually strategized over a response, and disagreements over the direction of the labor movement caused several key AFL–CIO affiliates to join with the

Service Employees International Union (SEIU) to break away and form a new federation called the Change to Win Federation (CTW) in 2005. The CTW did not keep all of its affiliates as time passed, with the United Carpenters and Joiners Union of America leaving in 2009, but the SEIU and the International Brotherhood of Teamsters (IBT) stayed as founding unions and they each had over a million members. CTW would later rename itself the Strategic Organizing Center.[29] Divisions in the movement made it difficult to mount a collective policy response to a free-market corporate agenda. Corporations continued to be more united and have larger resources than unions, and it was remarkable that labor was able to maintain political influence during the years of the second Bush administration.

The 2008 presidential election brought renewed hope to unions and to their members, and some trepidation for employers. Disillusionment with the wars in Iraq and Afghanistan and fury over the 2008 financial crisis led voters to elect Democrat Barack Obama as president, and to give Democrats even greater control over Congress including a super-majority in the Senate. Unions wanted Obama to devote political capital to passaging the Employee Free Choice Act, which would have made it easier to organize new workplaces, and the bill did pass through the House of Representatives but could not overcome a filibuster in the Senate.[30]

Obama was able to get the Affordable Care Act (ACA) through Congress, and the ACA had a major impact on all American workers. It can be regarded as an employment bill because health-care coverage is so inextricably linked to a person's job in the United States and it also had a major impact on how the American health-care industry operates, which is important as there are over 8 million Americans employed as health-care practitioners and technicians.[31] The sector is not highly unionized, with less than 15 percent of American health-care practitioners represented by unions in 2022.[32] Any change to the way that health care operates in the United States ultimately impacts work and employment in the United States.

American Management in 2000s

The growth of platform capitalism markedly shaped the United States and global economies in the 2000s. As Shoshanna Zuboff has shown, companies like Google (now Alphabet), Facebook, Amazon, Apple, and even Microsoft relied on a new business model that turned the people using their services into commodities.[33] For example, Facebook charged nobody using social media platform but monitored and shaped the behavior of users – the social media term for people – and turned that data into a marketable product. Facebook and other platforms were able to target advertising content at consumers in a way that had not been possible in prior decades. New platform capitalism corporations did not employ many workers compared with their predecessors in earlier decades. For instance, Google only had 22,000 employees in 2009.[34] Those companies were wildly profitable, with Google stock worth $353 per share in that same year.[35] Firms like Google, Amazon, and Facebook were non-union and their management sought to remain that way.

Older established firms went through a major change in the 2000s. This was most notably seen when GM and Chrysler went into bankruptcy protection and together received a $17.4 billion bailout from the US government.[36] The governments of Canada and Ontario also contributed to the bailout. Ford was the only one of the three Detroit automakers that did not seek government assistance. This was the second time that Chrysler was bailed-out – the first Chrysler bail-out was in 1979 – and GM was popularly and derisively called Government Motors because it received government assistance. The major Japanese and European automakers operating in the United States and Canada did not go through bankruptcy restructuring as they did not need it. Industrial workers in the United States were again faced with demands for management concessions as a result of the 2008 economic crisis. The Detroit automakers forced two-tier wage agreements on their workers, and the same type of policy was pursued in Canada.

Canadian Unions in the 2000s

Canadian unions continued to be more influential than their American counterparts as they entered the twenty-first century, but nonetheless faced significant challenges. The Progressive Conservative government in Ontario was led by premier Ernie Eves when it was defeated by the provincial Liberal party led by Dalton McGuinty in 2004. The Ontario Liberals adopted a more conciliatory approach to unions than their predecessors but did not fully restore the progressive labor and employment laws implemented by the Rae government in the early 1990s.

Federal public sector unions faced the most anti-labor government formed in Canada in the modern political era with the Harper government in power. The labor movement managed to mount a more coherent and unified response to neo-liberal social and economic policy than its American counterpart. This was seen during the 2001 Summit of the Americas meeting in Québec City. Major Canadian unions and the Canadian Labor Congress (CLC) leadership led activists from across the country to demonstrate at the summit, although it was not brought to a stop like the WTO meeting in Seattle. From the perspective of the author of this book, who was at the Summit of the Americas protest, labor's presence at Québec City was perhaps too peaceful and may have been more effective had it joined the radical protestors who faced teargas in the old town in the city.

There were major labor disputes in the 2000s, and public sector unions figured prominently in them. For example, there was growing militancy in higher education and more generally in elementary and secondary education. Jobs actions included a long strike by contract faculty and teaching assistants at York University from 2008 to 2009. OPSEU went on strike in 2002, and there were two Toronto Transit Commission strikes in 2006 and 2008. Canada Post workers went on strike in 2011, and teachers in British Columbia in 2005 and 2014. There were many other struggles across the country, and fighting against employer austerity measures was central to all of those strikes. Union density declined a few percentage points during the 2000s because of the wave of industrial job losses that occurred but was still far more robust than in the United States.[37]

Canadian Management in the 2000s

Management tends to alternate between celebrating what it collectively considers successes and issuing dire warnings of what could happen to the economy if its dictums are not closely followed. It is overall a method of creating useful anxiety among workers and other stakeholders, except shareholders, who are external to a firm. There is a common saying among managers that a good crisis should never be wasted, and the 2000s brought useful crises. Naomi Campbell and others have used the term Disaster Capitalism to describe how business exploits crises for maximum gain, and this practice was entirely evident during and after 2008.[38]

Corporations used the 2008 financial crisis to lay-off hundreds of thousands of workers across Canada, with 400,000 jobs lost in the year following October 2008.[39] Unemployment increased by 31 percent between 2008 and 2010.[40] Those increases were not as great as what occurred during the 1981 and 1990 recessions but were nonetheless a difficult experience for Canadian workers. A principal challenge was the growing use of contract workers and third-party agencies to staff corporations. The centrality of temporary employment agencies, whose workers are extremely difficult to unionize, became quite apparent by the end of the 2000s. Whereas it was an exception to see firms like Adecco and Kelly appearing at college and university recruitment fairs following prior recessions, such firms became fixtures in the job market by the end of the decade. Temporary agency work became a way for new workers to enter the job market, and for displaced workers to re-enter it.

Canada was different from the United States in the 2000s when it came to the firms and sectors that were central to the country's economy. There were some major Canadian Internet and telecommunication technology firms. Research In Motion, the firm that created the Blackberry phone, was the most widely known of them during the 2000s. A key problem was that Canadian firms that became successful in areas of emerging technology either failed or were taken over by foreign companies. For example, Corel was considered a potential competitor for Microsoft but eventually became owned by an American investment firm. Major manufacturing firms like Bombardier, Magna, and Linamar operated as Canadian-owned but, as Canada is a middle power, it was difficult for Canadian firms to compete with larger overseas firms.

Some basic differences between Canadian and American management practices persisted into the 2000s, with language continuing to be a major distinction between both countries. There were some caveats when it came to managing in English and French Canada. Working in a firm like Bombardier, headquartered in Montréal, required fluency in both French and English. A manager in the Québec civil service or in a publicly owned corporation like Hydro Québec did not require familiarity with English. There was greater likelihood that a manager in English Canada would be conversant in only English, unless employed in the federal public service.

The gender composition of management continued to change during the 2000s, although there was little diversity in terms of race and ethnicity. Being a manager in the 2000s in Canada was a precarious occupation, even though management collectively had disproportionate influence over labor–management relations. Individual managers had less legal protection than the people whom they supervised, especially if the people reporting to them were unionized. Managers were often not covered by the same employment standards regulations and labor laws as other workers. For example, managers were often not eligible for overtime pay, and could be expected to work virtually unlimited numbers of hours every week. Managers could only pursue unjust workplace treatment through lawsuits against their employers, and taking that path often proved insurmountably difficult. Non-union employees

Table 4.1 Union Density Percentage in the United States and Canada, 1990 and 2010

	1990	*2010*
Canada	35.4	30
United States	16.1	11.9

Source: Diane Galarneau and Thao Sohn, "Long Term Trends in Unionization," *Statistics Canada*, 20 May 2022, www150.statcan.gc.ca/n1/pub/75-006-x/2013001/arti cle/11878-eng.htm#a3; The Economics Daily, "Union Membership Rate 10.5 Percent in 2018, Down from 20.1 Percent in 1983," *US Bureau of Labor Statistics*, 25 January 2019, www.bls.gov/opub/ted/2019/union-membership-rate-10-point-5-percent-in-2018-down-from-20-point-1-percent-in-1983.htm

could sue for wrongful dismissal in Canada, but it is challenging to substantiate such a charge in court. Managers can be held legally liable for health and safety incidents on the job, although there is usually little risk of being incarcerated even in the event that a worker is killed.

A New Millennium with the Same Challenges

The 2000s ended with the United States and Canada struggling to emerge from a global financial crisis. Deindustrialization worsened in both countries, precarious work became more prevalent, and the Canadian and American political climates were difficult as Republicans and Conservatives led national governments. Management seemed to have even more power when it came to dealing with workers, and companies still benefited from having access to an excess supply of labor. New companies that were non-union and hostile toward worker organizing became dominant, with established unionized firms like GM facing huge challenges. As Table 4.1 shows, there was ongoing divergence between Canadian and American unions as the former held ground, at least in Canada, while the latter continued to decline. Labor and employment law had not been adequately reformed in either country to reflect the emerging realities of twenty-first-century employment. The 12 years from 2010 to 2022 brought some surprises that were alternatively enormously helpful and grievously harmful.

Notes

1 Commission on the Future of Worker–Management Relations, U.S., "The Dunlop Commission on the Future of Worker–Management Relations – Final Report" (Washington: 1 December 1994).

2 Commission on the Future of Worker–Management Relations, 92.
3 World Trade Organization, "History of the Multi-lateral Trading System," 5 May 2022, www.wto.org/english/thewto_e/history_e/history_e.htm.
4 Thomas Piketty, *Capital in the Twenty-First Century* (Cambridge: Belknap, 2014).
5 Isaac Cohen, "The Caterpillar Labor Dispute and the UAW, 1991–1998," *Labor Studies Journal*, 27, no. 4 (Winter 2003): 79.
6 Cohen, "The Caterpillar Labor Dispute," 82.
7 Ibid., 83.
8 For an account of the Caterpillar strike, see Ibid., 77–99.
9 International Brotherhood of Teamsters, "Judge Approves Agreement Ending Government Oversight of Teamsters Union," 18 February 2015, https://teamster.org/2015/02/judge-approves-agreement-ending-governm ent-oversight-teamsters-union/.
10 Teamsters for a Democratic Union, "Ron Carey: Visionary Teamster Leader Dies at 72," 12 December 2008, www.tdu.org/news_ron-carey-vision ary-teamster-leader-dies-72.
11 Teamsters for a Democratic Union, www.tdu.org/news_ron-carey-vision ary-teamster-leader-dies-72.
12 Matt Weyrich, "MLB Work Stoppages: History of Lockouts, Strikes in Baseball," *NBC Sports*, 13 March 2022, www.nbcsports.com/washington/ nationals/mlb-work-stoppages-history-lockouts-strikes-baseball.
13 W. Edwards Deming, *Out of the Crisis* (Cambridge: Massachusetts Institute of Technology, Centre for Advanced Engineering Study, 1986).
14 Mel Van Elteren, *Managerial Control of American Workers: Methods and Technology from the 1880s to Today* (Jefferson: McFarland, 2017), 145.
15 Susan M. Heathfield, "Society for Human Resource Management – SHRM," *The Balance Careers*, 20 August 2019, www.thebalancecareers. com/society-for-human-resource-management-shrm-1918261.
16 See Bob Rae, *From Protest to Power: Personal Reflections on a Life in Politics* (Toronto: Penguin, 1997) for an account of the Ontario NDP's term in power.
17 Sid Ryan, *A Grander Vision: My Life in the Labour Movement* (Toronto: Dundurn, 2019), 119–154.
18 *Ontario Labor Relations Act*, 15 April 2022, www.ontario.ca/laws/statute/ 95l01#BK1.
19 Alberta Economic Development Authority. *Joint Review Committee Right-to-Work Study Final Report* (Edmonton: 30 November 1995).
20 *Many Rivers to Cross*, directed by Michael Ostroff (1999; Ottawa: Canadian Union of Postal Workers) is one of the most insightful films on collective bargaining as it is about contentious 1997 negotiations between CUPW and Canada Post Corporation.
21 *Lavigne v. Ontario Public Service Employees Union*. 2 S.C.R. 211 (1991).

22 James Rinehart, Christopher Huxley, David Robertson, *Just Another Car Factory? Lean Production and Its Discontents* (Ithaca: Cornell ILR Press, 1997) is a full analysis of what led to labor–management conflict at CAMI.

23 *National Labor Relations Board v. Kentucky River Community Care, Inc.*, 532 U.S. 706 (2001). See Jean-Christian Vinel, *The Employee: A Political History* (Philadelphia: University of Pennsylvania Press, 2013), 1–9 for comment on *Kentucky River* and background on the politics of defining who is an employee.

24 Council of Economic Advisors, "Economic Report of the President," 108th Congress, 2nd Session. H. Doc. 108–145 (Washington, DC: United States Government Printing Office, 2004), 73–74.

25 David E. Sanger with Stephen Greenhouse, "President Invokes Taft–Hartley Act to Open 29 Ports," *New York Times*, 9 October 2002, www.nytimes.com/2002/10/09/us/president-invokes-taft-hartley-act-to-open-29-ports.html.

26 Timothy J. Minchin, *Labor Under Fire: A History of the AFL–CIO Since 1979* (Chapel Hill: University of North Carolina Press, 2017), 264–265.

27 Minchin, *Labor Under Fire,* 272.

28 Ibid., 271.

29 Strategic Organizing Center, "Power at Work," 15 May 2022, https://thesoc.org/.

30 Cornell ILR School, "Employee Free Choice Act," 16 May 2022, www.ilr.cornell.edu/news/about-ilr/employee-free-choice-act.

31 United States Bureau of Labor Statistics, "Occupational Employment and Wages, May 2021, 29-0000 Healthcare Practitioners and Technical Occupations (Major Group)," 16 May 2022, www.bls.gov/oes/current/oes290000.htm.

32 United States Bureau of Labor Statistics, "Union Members – 2021," *US Department of Labor*, 20 January 2022, www.bls.gov/news.release/pdf/union2.pdf.

33 See Shoshana Zuboff, *The Age of Surveillance Capitalism: The Fight for a Human Future at the New Frontier of Power* (New York: Public Affairs, 2019) for a disturbing and insightful analysis of platform capitalism companies.

34 Catherine Clifford, "Layoffs Hit Google: 200 Jobs Cuts," *CNN Money*, 26 March 2002, https://money.cnn.com/2009/03/26/technology/google_layoffs/index.htm.

35 Clifford, "Layoffs Hit Google."

36 Mike Allen and David Rogers, "Bush Announces $17.4 Billion Auto Bailout," *Politico*, 19 December 2008, www.politico.com/story/2008/12/bush-announces-174-billion-auto-bailout-016740.

37 Industrial Relations and Human Resources Library, "Canadian Strikes," *University of Toronto*, 20 May 2022, https://guides.library.utoronto.ca/c.php?g=250906&p=1680318.

38 See Naomi Klein, *The Shock Doctrine: The Rise of Disaster Capitalism* (Toronto: A.A. Knopf, 2007).

39 Canadian Broadcasting Corporation News, "Recession Job Losses Not so Bleak: StatsCan," 23 February 2011, www.cbc.ca/news/business/recession-job-losses-not-so-bleak-statscan-1.1003209.

40 CBC News, "Recession Job Losses Not so Bleak: StatsCan."

Conclusion and Looking Forward

This book endeavored to cover a lot of ground in a relatively short amount of space by discussing key trends and events in the history of labor–management conflict in the United States and Canada. Some of them involve labor and employment law, how labor–management interaction has been structured, technological change, economic policy, and political and social differences between both countries. Labor and management in both countries entered the 1930s without much of a legal framework to guide interaction in the workplace. Canada had the Industrial Disputes Investigation Act (IDIA) but it reflected a voluntaristic form of labor–management interaction and did not compel both sides in a dispute to engage in collective bargaining. American unions had to cope with a legal environment that could make them liable for damages during a work stoppage. The brief rapprochement between labor and management that happened during the World War I ended in 1919, and there was a wave of employer militancy against unions.

The Wagner framework introduced in the United States in 1935 in unique social, economic, and political circumstances, revolutionized labor–management interaction. Unions wanted legal collective bargaining and for workers to have the right to form labor organizations of their own choosing without interference from employers. Canadian workers knew what was happening south of the border during the New Deal years and also wanted a legal framework like the Wagner Act, and they eventually got it in 1944 with the introduction of PC 1003. They also joined American-based industrial unions in huge numbers. The only real exception to the Wagner-based system in Canada was found in the federal public service, where the Whitley-based industrial council was also formalized in 1944 with the creation of the National Joint Council even though it had been informally used since right after World War I.

DOI: 10.4324/9780429294938-6

Management practices in Canada and the United States were similar in the 1930s and 1940s when it came to operating corporations, but the South was unique due to anti-labor policy in that region that was heavily shaped by racism. There was some variation in union density across Canada by the end of the 1940s, but Canada has never had an anti-union region like the American South. The South was politically powerful, and racist anti-union animus was prevalent among Democrats and later by Republicans in the South. The existence of so much anti-unionism in the South is one of the key differences between Canada and the United States. Barry Eidlin has argued that the difference between unionization rates in Canada and the United States can be attributed to Canadian workers facing more hostility from the state, which in turn led to greater working-class identity, while American workers and unions were co-opted by the state and thus there was less class identity manifested in the United States. There may be merit to that view but thinking about class in terms of the workplace means devoting equal analysis to managerial class identity, which clearly influenced labor–management interaction.[1]

Party politics is another major difference between the two countries. American political parties are often described as "big tents" that include many different factions, and both the Democrats and the Republicans underwent significant change from the time that they were founded until the early twentieth century. The Republicans changed from being the party of Free Soil, Free Labor, Free Men when the party was founded in 1854, and advocates for the abolition of slavery, to being the party of big business after the US Civil War. The party's pro-business orientation became a defining aspect of its ideology. The Democrats faced internal division over slavery, but gradually became the party of labor by the early twentieth century. The New Deal made labor a key constituent in the party, although labor's influence over party policy weakened as union density declined following the 1960s. There are other parties on election ballots in the United States, but the two main parties dominate the electoral process and have endeavored to ensure that it is difficult for third-party candidates to be competitive.

Canada achieved independence from the United Kingdom in 1867 with a two-party system of Liberals and Conservatives, and it became a three-party system with the creation of the Cooperative Commonwealth Federation (CCF) in 1932. The CCF and its New Democratic Party (NDP) successor never formed a national government but were instrumental in implementing key social programs in Canada, along with passing legislation at the provincial level that is pro-labor. The existence of the CCF and NDP also drew the Liberals leftward at key moments, such as with the introduction of the Canada Pension Plan and universal health care, although the Liberals have generally shown themselves to be ideologically flexible. In contrast, the Conservative party in Canada now makes no pretense of even being slightly to the right of the center of the political spectrum and instead has become a right-wing populist movement.

Labor and employment law is a third defining difference between Canada and the United States. Canada indeed adopted much of the Wagner system in the late 1940s, but the *Snider* decision ensured that the system had its main influence at the provincial rather than federal level. Wagner also undergirds the Canada Labor Code – the law that regulates labor–management interaction in federally regulated industries – but there is a contrast with the United States because the Wagner Act has national rather than state-level authority. Public sector workers in both countries are covered by provincial and state laws, but there is more variation in how those laws function in the United States than in Canada. There are states where public sector workers face severe barriers to unionization, and such a prohibition does not exist in Canada. The right of public sector workers to strike is also more severely curtailed in the United States. While there have been major strikes in both countries, conflicts in the public sector have at times been more pronounced than in the private sector. Governments in both countries have enormous power over unionized workers, both as employer and legislator, and have not hesitated to use it. The way that courts in the United States and Canada have approached labor issues, especially the US Supreme Court and the Supreme Court of Canada, is an especially important point of divergence that impacts labor–management interaction. The US Supreme Court became increasingly anti-union and anti-worker during the 1990s and subsequent decades, while the Supreme Court of Canada has interpreted the Charter of Rights and Freedoms to expand labor rights.

Declines in union density in the United States have led to the American labor movement essentially being a regional movement that claims a national mandate. Spring 2022 data from the US Bureau of Labor Statistics showed that 10.3 percent of American workers were unionized and 30 percent of union members live in two states: California and New York. There were 14 million union members in the United States in 2021, and they were evenly divided between the public and private sectors. This means that 6.1 percent of private sector workers were in unions, with 33.9 percent of public sector workers unionized.[2]

The situation in Canada in 2021 showed some of the same trends found in the United States, but with organized labor in a stronger position than its American counterpart. The overall density rate is higher with 30.9 percent of Canadian workers belonging to unions with 77.2 of public employees and 15.3 percent of private sector workers in unions, and five-million workers covered by union membership. The overall unionization rate in Canada was consequently three times higher than in the United States in 2021. The US population is nine times larger than Canada's. That fact certainly illustrates the strength of the Canadian labor movement, but it also shows a challenge that equally faces labor in both countries. There is room for unions to expand in the American public sector, but public sector employment has never been as large as work in the private sector. In Canada, virtually every public sector worker who can be in a union belongs to one. Public sector employment levels in both countries are not expanding compared with the private sector. This led to the Canadian and American labor movements being essentially public sector movements. Unions will have to find better methods of organizing private sector workers, especially in the United States, if they want to become more economically, socially, and politically relevant.[3]

The 2010s and the early years of the 2020s brought new and unexpected challenges for organizations of all types and the workers and managers who were employed in them. Changes in labor and employment law in Canada and the United States were a major theme in this 12-year period, as was further political change. Changes in the nature of the employment relationship were discussed in public discourse as the gig economy led people to wonder what it meant to be an employee as the twenty-first century progressed. Electoral politics had a profound impact from 2010 to 2022, with politics in the United States becoming especially polarized. This period ended with all countries dealing with a worldwide pandemic, which had a major impact on work and employment although not to the extent often suggested in the popular media. Those years ended with signs of improvement for labor and evidence of new challenges for management. The short period from 2020 to 2022, which is still in progress at the time this book was written, has had a particularly important impact on the interaction between employers and workers.

The United States in the 2010s

The United States federally was governed for most of this decade by Barack Obama leading a Democratic administration in the White House and an increasingly reactionary Republican party controlling Congress and a majority of state governor's mansions and legislatures.

For organized labor, the real change in the labor–management system came at the state rather than the federal level. Right-to-Work laws had long been regarded as a problem that was specific to the South and parts of the mid-West. Republicans began winning elections in states in the 2010s where they had not previously been dominant, and one of the first things that they did was push Right-to-Work laws through legislatures as quickly as they could.

Right-to-Work was passed in Michigan, Indiana, and Wisconsin, which were all states that were once considered reliably Democratic. The situation in Wisconsin was especially instructive as it showed the determination of the twenty-first-century Republican party to make it impossible to organize unions. Governor Scott Walker built a national profile on attacks on organized labor, and he made it clear that he was using a "divide and conquer" strategy to attack Wisconsin unions.[4] Walker was largely successful as union density in Wisconsin dropped from 14.1 percent in 2011 to 9.3 percent in 2021.[5]

Right-to-Work was not the sole cause of union decline in Wisconsin, as the 2011 Wisconsin Budget Repair Bill also required public sector unions to recertify as bargaining representatives every year while only permitting them to negotiate over base wages.[6] Indiana, a state that once also had high union density introduced Right-to-Work in 2010. It had 10 percent union density that year, and the rate was the same in 2021.[7] Michigan also passed a Right-to-Work law in 2012, but its union density only dropped from 17.1 percent that year to 15.3 percent in 2021.[8] The problem with Right-to-Work is that there were workers who were covered by union collective agreement and then a smaller percentage who were actually paying union dues. In the case of Michigan in 2021, there were 620,000 workers covered by collective agreements with 540,000 actually being dues-paying members.

The challenge with Right-to-Work was worsened when the US Supreme Court issued its *Janus v. AFSCME* decision in 2018. Mark Janus, a public employee in Illinois, objected to paying union dues on the premise that his right to freedom of speech under the US Constitution. This was a challenge to the *Abood v Detroit Board of Education* decision, and lower courts were clear that they could not overrule the earlier decision and that the Supreme Court would have to consider Janus's case. The court, in a 5–4 decision written by Justice Samuel Alito, indeed sided with Janus and in the process implemented Right-to-Work across all American public sector workplaces.[9] Some states, such as New York and California, took pre-emptive steps to protect public sector labor rights in anticipation of the court ruling in favor of Janus. The *Janus* decision worried American unions and was cheered by the political right but, as of 2022, it has not yet had the catastrophic impact on public sector union coverage that was feared in 2018. The public sector union membership rate in the United States was 33.9 percent in 2018, and it was also the same rate in 2021.[10]

Canada in the 2010s

Canadian workers experienced a wave of plant closures and deindustrialization following the 2008 recession. One case, the closure of a locomotive plant in London, Ontario, symbolized the peril unions faced when confronting corporations that operated on a global scale and could pit workers in higher wage jurisdictions against their counterparts in low-wage regions and countries. The London plant, called Electromotive, was owned by Caterpillar and the company once again used the same tough tactics that it employed against the UAW in the 1990s. The Canadian Auto Workers fought the closure but were unable to keep the plant open. The closure attracted international media attention and represented a wider pattern of job loss across the country.[11]

Labor rights took a different direction through decisions from the Supreme Court of Canada. As Larry Savage and Charles Smith have noted, unions have increasingly turned to the courts to protect labor rights.[12] The court issued decisions in the 2010s that amazed even the most optimist labor activists. In 2007, the court had already ruled that workers have a right to engage in collective bargaining in the *Health Services and Support – Facilities Subsector Bargaining Assn. v. British Columbia (BC Health Services)* decision.[13] The court had also ruled in 2001 that agricultural workers had a right to unionize.[14] Those two rulings were followed in 2015 with the *Saskatchewan Federation of Labour v. Saskatchewan* decision which said that the right to strike is constitutionally protected, and the 2015 *Mounted Police Association of Ontario v. Canada* decision that affirmed the right to unionize.[15] In that latter case, members of the Royal Canadian Mounted Police had been prohibited from unionizing like their counterparts in other police services, and the court extended the right to them.

It was clear by the end of the 2010s that the supreme courts of Canada and the United States were on entirely different trajectories as the former expanded labor rights while the latter overturned long-standing precedent to weaken unions and strengthen the position of employers in the workplace. It is problematic for Canadian unions that union membership is not expanding even though the Supreme Court of Canada has said that there is a right to unionization. The nature of the labor relations framework beyond court decisions is the main problem facing unions. Certifying a union still requires a two-step process of firstly having prospective members sign union membership cards, then submitting those cards to a labor relations board to prove that an election should be held to formally create a local union. Most Canadian jurisdictions permit certification based on cards – known as card-check certification – but a minimum threshold must be met in order for that to occur and that threshold is usually well beyond a simple majority of potential members signing cards. Only federal labor law in Canada stipulates that a simple majority of workers need to sign cards in order for a union to be certified.

The political situation in Canada was mixed for unions and employers in the 2010s. The federal Conservative government was generally hostile toward organized labor and oriented to the interests of business. For example, 8,600 workers at Air Canada were poised to strike in 2012 and the Harper Conservatives pre-emptively passed back to work legislation before the workers had actually gone on strike.[16] The government took a similar approach in 2016 when Canada Post workers were locked out by their employer after engaging in rotating strikes.[17] Such moves ultimately strengthened the position of management when dealing with labor.

Canada is also now home to organizations that promote anti-union policy and support corporations during workplace disputes. For example, the Fraser Institute has long advocated for the introduction of Right-to-Work laws in Canada even though such laws would immediately face a constitutional challenge.[18] An organization called Labor Watch Canada disseminates anti-union information online.[19] London, Ontario firm Corporate Investigation Services provides surveillance of workers and security for employers during strikes.[20] The Canadian anti-union apparatus is not nearly as large as its American counterpart, but it is nonetheless actively trying to influence conflict between labor and management.

Canadian unions and their members are not organized around a unified political program to challenge anti-union political and economic sentiment. Most recently, a number of building trades unions endorsed the Conservative Party in the 2022 Ontario provincial election, even though that party has contentious relations with public sector unions due to the imposition of limits on public sector wage increases.[21] One union, the Christian Labor Association of Canada (CLAC), has long eschewed workplace confrontation and demonstrated an affinity for conservative public policy.[22]

Who Is an Employee in the Twenty-First Century?

Silicon Valley had given the United States and the world products and services in the first decades of the twenty-first century devised by new and dominant firms, and they tried to transform the nature of the modern workplace. This process frequently involved altering existing industries, and the seemingly large and innocuous taxi and limousine industry was one of them. Driving a taxi or limousine was never highly compensated work in the United States and Canada, but there were unionized firms in the business and a decent standard of living could be earned by unionized drivers. Taxis and limousines also usually had to be licensed by the municipalities in which they operated, and people could not legally just start driving around calling themselves a taxi service. That all began to quickly change in 2009.

Uber was founded in San Francisco in 2009 and it quickly evolved into a service that permitted virtually any car to be used in place of a taxi or other existing type of hire car service. A smartphone application was used by drivers to receive ride requests sent directly by Uber users, and transactions involved no cash. The taxi and limousine industry was soon reeling from the impact of Uber. The issue for Uber drivers in this arrangement was that Uber considered them to be independent contractors, even though they were all compelled to work under terms unilaterally and uniformly set by the company.

As David Doorey describes, there are three legal classifications of worker in Canada: employees, dependent contractors, and independent contractors.[23] A dependent contractor is legally much like an employee and is dependent on one or two employers for work. Uber has strenuously argued before the courts that its drivers are in fact contractors. The Supreme Court of Canada moved toward legally classifying Uber drivers as employees in a 2020 ruling on Uber's mandatory arbitration terms.[24] The issue of how Uber drivers, and indeed many gig economy workers, are classified is still not resolved as the 2020s progress.

American courts and legislatures have also wrestled with the legal ambiguity of gig workers, with California at the forefront of the debate. That state is a Democratic bastion and attempted to improve gig worker legal protection in 2019 by passing a law that was intended to force companies like Uber to classify their drivers as employees. The companies that would be impacted by the law responded by funding a ballot initiative called Proposition 22 – such initiatives are permitted under state law – that would keep workers like those at Uber and Lyft in independent contractor status while receiving limited employment benefits from the companies. Unions and affected workers responded by suing the companies in court, and a judge overturned Proposition 22 in 2021 as a violation of the California state constitution. The matter has yet to be definitively decided by an appeals court.[25]

The Coronavirus Pandemic

The Coronavirus pandemic, also known as the COVID-19 pandemic, that began in 2020 has had a significant impact on workplaces around the world although it is being mistakenly portrayed in many media reports as a pivotal shift in how employers interact with workers. The immediate impact of the pandemic was for organizations to send as many workers home from their offices as possible while still maintaining operations. Media coverage of people working from home during the pandemic, which was seeming to subside by mid-2022, often gave the impression that working from home was a widespread phenomenon that would radically transform how people worked and lived. The reality was quite different, as at best 40 percent of people could work from home at least part of the time while everyone else in the labor force had to be in a physical work location.[26]

The pandemic instead reinforced long-standing trends in workplace relations in Canada and the United States; indeed globally. It showed a continuing divide between workers in well-compensated skilled jobs who were able to use technology to work from home and keep themselves comparatively safe from exposure to COVID-19, and a larger group of workers who were in less skilled and poorly compensated work that required them to be on the job even though it was a threat to their personal safety. The pandemic also led to the accelerated use of surveillance technology to monitor people working from home and in physical employer locations.[27]

The labor and employment law frameworks in both countries mostly proved suited to addressing workplace disputes that arose because of the pandemic. Discipline and dismissal cases over worker compliance with rules governing the wearing of personal protective equipment to mitigate COVID-19 transmission and vaccination requirements were handled by labor boards and civil court decisions will eventually be issued on those issues. Labor boards have generally found that employers should negotiate with unions over COVID-19 protection measures, but that there is also a requirement to maintain workplace safety. Unions overwhelmingly sought protection for their members throughout the pandemic and unionized workers were often in environments where they could be exposed to the virus.

Low-wage workers at places like Amazon are aware that they were not always well-treated by their employers during the worst periods of the pandemic, they already knew that they worked in demanding conditions before the pandemic started, and they responded by forming unions in 2022. Workers at a huge Amazon fulfillment center on Staten Island, New York stunned the business community by forming the Amazon Labor Union despite the company's relentless efforts to dissuade them from unionizing.[28] Workers at Starbucks across the United States are also forming local unions and are doing so while company management pours millions of dollars into efforts to stop unionization.[29]

The Way Ahead

There has not been a global health emergency like the Coronavirus pandemic since the 1918 Influenza pandemic. That latter event claimed tens of millions of lives, yet it became a footnote in the history of the World War I. The 2020–2022 pandemic may loom large in popular consciousness in the coming decades, or it may occupy the same place in history as its 1918 predecessor. The trends in workplace relations that accelerated in the 2010s and during the pandemic will continue. Demographic change was becoming a challenge for employers by the 2010s as the baby boom generation began to retire. Low birth rates in the United States and Canada have led to a tight post-pandemic labor market with workers having more leverage when applying for jobs.

Current National Labor Relations Board General Counsel Jennifer Abruzzo is actively working to make it easier to unionize. For instance, she is urging the board to readopt the *Joy Silk* doctrine that would make it possible in certain circumstances for unions to claim they have the right to represent workers without having to hold elections.[30] The Biden administration supports the passage of a labor law reform bill called the Protecting the Right to Organize Act, but there is little chance of it getting past a Republican filibuster in the US Senate.[31] In Canada, the federal NDP has demanded, as a condition of minority government support, that the Liberals ban the use of replacement workers during strikes and lockouts in federally regulated industries.[32] The federal government is also introducing changes to the Canada Labor Code that will implement measures to improve conditions for people employed in precarious work, improve work–life balance, and a series of other changes.[33] The legislative front is not entirely positive for unions and workers despite these recent successes. For example, the government of Ontario passed legislation to cover gig workers that is little different than California's Proposition 22.[34]

Labor and employment law legislation will continue to lag emerging workplace trends. For organized labor, there is also problem of facing employers that are constantly evolving while unions have not been able to adapt quickly enough by changing their structures and tactics. The internal complexity of unions comes largely from their political and cultural dynamics, while their formal internal functions are comparatively basic in nature. They principally focus on representing members in workplaces and engaging in different forms of advocacy. Organizing new workers is secondary to those other functions. In contrast, while corporations are always focused on making money, they are constantly devising new forms and practices to achieve that objective.

The Wagner-based labor relations systems in Canada and the United States needs reform, but there is little likelihood that they will undergo fundamental change. For example, widespread sectoral bargaining – negotiating agreements that will cover workers across industries or economic sectors – will not soon become a feature of labor relations outside of the largely Whitley-based system that still exists for federal public employees in Canada. Some sectoral bargaining occurs in the construction industry but it is unlikely that manufacturing or service sector employers would accept it without a protracted struggle. Professional workers may well show greater interest in unionizing. The Canadian labor movement will probably remain larger and more viable than its American counterpart, since even minor reforms to the National Labor Relations Act have proven impossible to get through Congress in the face of Republican opposition. While labor and employment law needs updating in the United States and Canada, the situation is worse for American workers compared with their Canadian counterparts.

Issues of workplace surveillance will continue to grow in importance in the coming years. The ubiquity of algorithms makes it possible to collect enormous amounts of data about people on the job, and management will find it irresistible to make more extensive use of them. Differences between workers based on gender, race, ethnicity, identity, and other variables will be exacerbated as the chasm expands between highly skilled, well-paid work and jobs requiring less skill and offering lower pay. Conflict between labor and management will continue, although it will often involve unseen methods of employee resistance, such as trying to foil workplace surveillance systems, rather than formal unionization leading to strikes. If there is one certainty about the future of labor–management conflict in the United States and Canada it is that it will continue because workplaces are ultimately hierarchical. Workers have always rebelled against poor management practice and will continue to do so, while management will relentlessly strive to exert authority on the job.

Notes

1 Barry Eidlin, *Labor and the Class Idea in the United States and Canada* (Cambridge: Cambridge University Press, 2018).

2 United States Bureau of Labor Statistics, "Union Members 2021," *Bureau of Labor Statistics*, 20 January 2022, www.bls.gov/news.release/pdf/uni on2.pdf.

3 Statistics Canada, "Union Status by Industry," *Statistics Canada*, 7 January 2022, www150.statcan.gc.ca/t1/tbl1/en/tv.action?pid=1410013201; Statistics Canada, "Union Coverage by Industry, Monthly, Unadjusted for Seasonality," 6 May 2022, www150.statcan.gc.ca/t1/tbl1/en/tv.action?pid= 1410006901.

4 Painters DC30, "Scott Walker Admits to 'Divide and Conquer' Strategy, YouTube," 00:37, 31 May 2012, www.youtube.com/watch?v=EXc5 bBTA7wg.

5 United States Bureau of Labor Statistics, "Union Members in Wisconsin – 2021," *Bureau of Labor Statistics*, 16 March 2022, www.bls.gov/regions/ midwest/news-release/UnionMembership_Wisconsin.htm.

6 Joe Kelly, "Controversial Wisconsin Union Law Argued Anew at Seventh Circuit," *Courthouse News Service*, 13 November 2020, www.courthousen ews.com/controversial-wisconsin-union-law-argued-anew-at-seventh-circuit/.

7 United States Bureau of Labor Statistics, "Union Membership Historical Table for Indiana," *Bureau of Labor Statistics*, 27 April 2022, www.bls.gov/ regions/midwest/data/unionmembershiphistorical_indiana_table.htm.

8 United States Bureau of Labor Statistics, "Union Membership Historical Table for Michigan," *Bureau of Labor Statistics*, 27 April 2022, www. bls.gov/regions/midwest/data/unionmembershiphistorical_michigan_ta ble.htm.

9 *Janus v. American Federation of State, County, and Municipal Employees*, 585 U.S. (2018).

10 United States Bureau of Labor Statistics, "Union Members – 2021".

11 See Stephanie Ross and Jason Russell, "Caterpillar Hates Unions More than It Loves Profits," *Labour/Le Travail* (Spring 2018): 53–85.

12 Larry Savage and Charles W. Smith, *Unions in Court: Organized Labour and the Charter of Rights and Freedoms* (Vancouver: UBC Press, 2017), 3.

13 Savage and Smith, *Unions in Court*, 155.

14 Ibid., 4.

15 Ibid., 178.

16 The Canadian Press, "Air Canada Back-to-Work Bill Gets Royal Assent," *Canadian Broadcasting Corporation*, 15 March 2012, www.cbc.ca/news/ politics/air-canada-back-to-work-bill-gets-royal-assent-1.1268054.

17 Rachel Cardozo, "Ontario Judge Finds Back-to-Work Legislation Aimed at Postal Workers Violates Charter," *Can LII Connects*, 16 August 2016, https://canliiconnects.org/en/summaries/42968.

18 Niels Veldhuis and Jason Clemens, "To Remain Competitive, Ontario Needs to Follow Indiana and Michigan's Lead," *Fraser Institute*, 15 May 2022, www.fraserinstitute.org/article/remain-competitive-ontario-needs-fol low-indiana-and-michigans-lead.

19 Labor Watch Canada, 15 May 2022, http://labourwatch.com/.

20 Corporate Investigation Services, 15 May 2022, www.corporateinvestigati ons.com/.

21 Scott Hertz, "Division, Neglect Opens Door to Ford's Union Conquests," *Rankandfile.ca*, 23 May 2022, www.rankandfile.ca/ford-union-support/.

22 On CLAC see Steven Tufts and Mark Thomas, "The Christian Labor Association of Canada (CLAC): Between Company and Populist Unionism," *Labour/Le Travail*, 80 (Fall, 2017): 55–79.

23 David J. Doorey, *The Law of Work: Industrial Relations and Collective Bargaining* (Toronto: Emond, 2017), 18–19.

24 Olivia Stefanovich, "Supreme Court Sides with Uber Drivers, Opening Door to $400M Class-Action Lawsuit," 26 June 2020, www.cbc.ca/news/ politics/stefanovich-supreme-court-uber-class-action-decision-1.5626853.

25 Kate Conger and Kellen Browning, "A Judge Declared California's Gig Worker Law Unconstitutional. Now What?," *New York Times*, 23 August 2021, www.nytimes.com/2021/08/23/technology/california-gig-worker-law-explained.html.

26 Jason Russell, "What Will Work Look Like post-COVID-19? It Will Take Us Back to the Future," *Globe and Mail*, 11 April 2021, www.theg lobeandmail.com/opinion/article-what-will-work-look-like-post-covid-19-it-will-take-us-back-to-the/.

27 Zoë Corbyn, "'Bossware Is Coming for Almost Every Worker': The Software You Might Not Realize Is Watching You," *The Guardian*, 27 April 2022, www.theguardian.com/technology/2022/apr/27/remote-work-softw are-home-surveillance-computer-monitoring-pandemic.

28 Alex N. Press, "The Class War Is Raging at Amazon's Staten Island Complex," *Jacobin*, 25 April 2022, https://jacobinmag.com/2022/04/ama zon-labor-union-staten-island-ldj5-rally/.

29 Noam Scheiber, "Starbucks Union Campaign Pushes on, with at Least 16 Stores Now Organized," *New York Times*, 8 April 2022, www.nytimes.com/ 2022/04/08/business/economy/starbucks-union-new-york-vote.html.

30 Kate Bronfenbrenner, "Workers Can Win at Starbucks and Amazon and Beyond," *Jacobin*, 1 May 2022, www.jacobinmag.com/2022/05/union-victor ies-amazon-starbucks-nlrb-labor-law.

31 AFL–CIO, "What Is the PRO Act?," 25 May 2022, https://aflcio.org/pro-act.

32 Sarah Ritchie, "Federal NDP, Unions Happy Liberals Will Include Strikes in Anti-scab Law," *Toronto Star*, 29 March 2022, www.thestar.com/politics/ 2022/03/29/federal-ndp-unions-happy-liberals-will-include-strikes-in-anti-scab-law.html.

33 Government of Canada, "Labour Program: Changes to the Canada Labour Code and Other Acts to Better Protect Workplaces," 30 May 2022, www.can ada.ca/en/employment-social-development/programs/laws-regulations/lab our/current-future-legislative.html.

34 Vanmala Subramanian, "How Uber Got almost Everything It Wanted in Ontario's Working for Workers Act," *Globe and Mail*, 25 May 2022, www. theglobeandmail.com/business/article-uber-gets-almost-everything-it-wants-in-doug-fords-working-for-workers/.

Bibliography

Adler, William. *Mollie's Job: A Story of Life and Work on the Global Assembly Line*. New York: Scribner, 2000.

AFL-CIO. "What Is the PRO Act?" 25 May 2022. https://aflcio.org/pro-act.

Aivalis, Christo. *The Constant Liberal: Pierre Trudeau, Organized Labour, and the Canadian Social Democratic Left*. Vancouver: UBC Press, 2018.

Alberta Economic Development Authority. *Joint Review Committee Right-to-Work Study Final Report*. Edmonton, 30 November 1995.

Allen, Mike and David Rogers. "Bush Announces $17.4 Billion Auto Bailout." *Politico*, 19 December 2008. www.politico.com/story/2008/12/bush-announces-174-billion-auto-bailout-016740.

Anastakis, Dimitry. *Auto Pact: Creating a Borderless North American Auto Industry, 1960–1971*. Toronto: University of Toronto Press, 2005.

Archives of Ontario. Canadian Manufacturers' Association Fonds. RG7-1-0-1881.1, Box B353713. W.H. Whiteman, CMA, to Ontario Minister of Labor Bette Stephenson, 16 September 1976.

Bank of Canada. "Inflation Calculator." Accessed 30 April 2022. www.bankofcanada.ca/rates/related/inflation-calculator/.

Barnard, John. *American Vanguard: The United Auto Workers during the Reuther Years, 1935–1970*. Detroit: Wayne State University Press, 2004.

Berle, Adolf. A. and Gardiner C. Means. *The Modern Corporation and Private Property*. New York: Columbia University, Council for Research in the Social Sciences, 1933.

Boyd, Gerald, R. "Teamsters Vote to Endorse Reagan." *New York Times*, 31 August 1984. Section A, Page 12.

Braverman, Harry. *Labor and Monopoly Capital: The Degradation of Work in the Twentieth Century*. New York: Monthly Review Press, 1974.

Bronfenbrenner, Kate. "Workers Can Win at Starbucks and Amazon and Beyond." *Jacobin*, 1 May 2022. www.jacobinmag.com/2022/05/union-victories-amazon-starbucks-nlrb-labor-law.

Canadian Broadcasting Corporation News. "Recession Job Losses Not so Bleak: StatsCan." 23 February 2011. www.cbc.ca/news/business/recession-job-losses-not-so-bleak-statscan-1.1003209.

Cardozo, Rachel. "Ontario Judge Finds Back-to-Work Legislation Aimed at Postal Workers Violates Charter." *Can LII Connects*, 16 August 2016. https://canliiconnects.org/en/summaries/42968.

Carew, Tony. *American Labour's Cold War Abroad: From Deep Freeze to Détente, 1945–1970.* Edmonton: Athabasca University Press, 2018.

Chandler, Alfred. *The Visible Hand: The Managerial Revolution in American Business.* Cambridge: Belknap, 1977.

Clark, Shannon. *The Making of the American Creative Class: New York's Cultural Workers and Twentieth-Century Consumer Capitalism.* New York: Oxford University Press, 2021.

Clifford, Catherine. "Layoffs Hit Google: 200 Jobs Cuts." *CNN Money*, 26 March 2002. https://money.cnn.com/2009/03/26/technology/google_layoffs/index.htm.

Cohen, Issac. "The Caterpillar Labor Dispute and the UAW, 1991–1998." *Labor Studies Journal*, 27, no. 4 (Winter 2003): 77–99.

Coleman, Charles J. "The Civil Service Reform Act of 1978: Its Meaning and Roots." *Labor Law Journal*, 31, no. 4 (April 1980): 200–209.

Commission on the Future of Worker-Management Relations. "The Dunlop Commission on the Future of Worker–Management Relations – Final Report." Washington: 1 December 1994.

Communications Workers of America v. Beck, 487 U.S. 735 (1988).

Conger, Kate and Kellen Browning, "A Judge Declared California's Gig Worker Law Unconstitutional. Now What?" *New York Times*, 23 August 2021. www.nytimes.com/2021/08/23/technology/california-gig-worker-law-explained.html.

Corbyn, Zoë . "'Bossware Is Coming for Almost Every Worker': The Software You Might Not Realize Is Watching You." *The Guardian*, 27 April 2022. www.theguardian.com/technology/2022/apr/27/remote-work-software-home-surveillance-computer-monitoring-pandemic.

Cornell ILR School. "Employee Free Choice Act." 16 May 2022. www.ilr.cornell.edu/news/about-ilr/employee-free-choice-act.

Corporate Investigation Services. 15 May 2022. www.corporateinvestigations.com/.

Cowie, Jefferson. *Capital Moves: RCA's Seventy-Year Quest for Cheap Labor.* Ithaca: Cornell University Press, 1999.

Cowie, Jefferson. *Stayin' Alive: The 1970s and the Last Days of the Working Class.* New York: The New Press, 2010.

Cowie, Jefferson. *The Great Exception: The New Deal and the Limits of American Politics.* Princeton: Princeton University Press, 2019.

Craig, Maggie. *When the Clyde Ran Red: A Social History of Red Clydeside.* Edinburgh: Berlinn, 2018. Deming, W. Edwards. *Out of the Crisis.* Cambridge: Massachusetts Institute of Technology, Centre for Advanced Engineering Study, 1986.

Derickson, Alan. "'Asleep and Awake at the Same Time': Sleep Denial among Pullman Porters." *Labor: Studies in Working-Class History of the America's*, 5, no. 3 (2008): 13–44.

Doellgast, Virginia and Chiara Benassi. "Collective Bargaining." In Adrian Wilkinson, et al., eds. *Handbook of Research on Employee Voice*. 227–246. Cheltenham: Edward Elgar, 2014.

Doorey, David J. *The Law of Work: Industrial Relations and Collective Bargaining*. Toronto: Emond, 2017.

Drucker, Peter. *The Practice of Management*. New York: Harper and Brothers, 1954.

Dubofsky, Melvyn. *The State and Labor in Modern America*. Chapel Hill: University of North Carolina Press, 1994.

Eidlin, Barry. *Labor and the Class Idea in the United States and Canada*. Cambridge: Cambridge University Press, 2018.

Emre, Merve. *The Personality Brokers: The Strange History of Myers-Briggs and the Birth of Personality Testing*. New York: Doubleday, 2018.

Endicott, Stephen L. *Raising the Workers' Red Flag: The Workers' Unity League of Canada, 1930–1936*. Toronto: University of Toronto Press, 2012.

Farber, David R. *Sloan Rules: Alfred P. Sloan and the Triumph of General Motors*. Chicago: University of Chicago Press, 2002.

Feurer, Rosemary and Chad Pearson, eds. "Introduction: Against Labor." In *Against Labor: How U.S. Employers Organized to Defeat Union Activism*. Urbana: University of Illinois Press, 2017.

Fones-Wolf, Elizabeth and Ken Fones-Wolf, *Struggle for the Soul of the Postwar South*. Urbana: University of Illinois Press, 2015.

Fudge, Judy and Eric Tucker. *Labour Before the Law: The Regulation of Workers' Collective Action in Canada, 1900–1948*. Toronto: Oxford University Press, 2001.

Galarneau, Diane and Thao Sohn. "Long Term Trends in Unionization." *Statistics Canada*, 20 May 2022. www150.statcan.gc.ca/n1/pub/75-006-x/2013001/article/11878-eng.htm#a3.

Galenson, David W. "The Rise and Fall of Indentured Servitude in the Americas: An Economic Analysis." *The Journal of Economic History*, 44, no. 1 (1983–4): 1–26.

Ganz, Marshall. *Why David Sometimes Wins: Leadership, Organization, and Strategy in the California Farm Worker Movement*. Oxford: Oxford University Press, 2009.

Gillespie, Richard. *Manufacturing Knowledge: A History of the Hawthorne Experiments*. Cambridge: Cambridge University Press, 1991.

Gindin, Sam. *The Canadian Auto Workers: The Birth and Transformation of a Union*. Toronto: Lorimer, 1995.

Gonick, Cy, Paul Phillips, and Jesse Vorst eds. *Labour Gains, Labour Pains: 50 Years of PC 1003*. Winnipeg: Fernwood, 1995.

Government of Canada. "Labour Program: Changes to the Canada Labour Code and Other Acts to Better Protect Workplaces." 30 May 2022. www.canada.ca/en/employment-social-development/programs/laws-regulations/labour/current-future-legislative.html.

Government of Ontario. "Ontario Labor Relations Act." 15 April 2022. www.ontario.ca/laws/statute/95l01#BK1.

Gray, David. *Work Better, Live Better: Motivation, Labor, and Management Ideology.* Amherst: University of Massachusetts Press, 2020.

Griffin, Kevin. "This Week in History: Bobby Orr Becomes First NHL 'Millionaire.'" *Vancouver Sun,* 25 August 2017. https://vancouversun.com/news/local-news/this-week-in-history-bobby-orr-becomes-first-nhl-mill ionaire.

Hannah-Jones, Nikole et al. eds. *The 1619 Project: A New Origin Story.* New York: One World, 2021.

Harris, Howell John. *The Right to Manage: Industrial Relations Policies of American Business in the 1940s.* Madison: University of Wisconsin, 1982.

Harris, Todd, dir. *Grace Hartman: The First Woman to Lead a Major Canadian Union.* Toronto: Labour Video Communications, 1997.

Heathfield, Susan M. "Society for Human Resource Management – SHRM." *The Balance Careers,* 20 August 2019. www.thebalancecareers.com/society-for-human-resource-management-shrm-1918261.

Heron, Craig. *Lunch-Bucket Lives: Remaking the Workers' City.* Toronto: Between the Lines, 2015.

Heron, Craig and Charles Smith. *The Canadian Labour Movement: A Short History,* third edition. Toronto: Lorimer, 2020.

Hogler, Raymond. *The End of American Unions: The Right-to-Work Movement and the Erosion of Collective Bargaining.* Denver: Praeger, 2015.

Hollander, Taylor. *Power, Politics, and Principles: Mackenzie King and Labour, 1935–1948.* Toronto: University of Toronto Press, 2018.

Hurd, Richard W. "Moving Beyond the Critical Synthesis: Does the Law Preclude a Future for US Unions?" *Labor History,* 54, no. 2 (2013): 193–200.

Industrial Relations and Human Resources Library. "Canadian Strikes." *University of Toronto,* 20 May 2022. https://guides.library.utoronto.ca/c.php?g=250906&p=1680318.

International Brotherhood of Teamsters. "Judge Approves Agreement Ending Government Oversight of Teamsters Union." 18 February 2015. https://teamster.org/2015/02/judge-approves-agreement-ending-government-oversi ght-teamsters-union/.

Jackson, Andrew. "BC Premier Dave Barrett Showed the Canadian Left How to Make Change Happen." *Jacobin,* 20 July 2021. www.jacobinmag.com/2021/07/british-columbia-dave-barrett-ndp-social-credit.

Jacoby, Sanford. *Modern Manors: Welfare Capitalism Since the New Deal.* Princeton: Princeton University Press, 1997.

Janus v. American Federation of State, County, and Municipal Employees, 585 U.S. (2018).

Kealey, Gregory S. *Toronto Workers Respond to Industrial Capitalism, 1867–1892.* Toronto: University of Toronto Press, 1980.

Kearney, Richard. *Labor Relations in the Public Sector,* fourth edition. New York: CRC Press, 2009.

Kelly, Joe. "Controversial Wisconsin Union Law Argued Anew at Seventh Circuit." *Courthouse News Service,* 13 November 2020. www.courthousen ews.com/controversial-wisconsin-union-law-argued-anew-at-seventh-circuit/.

Keynes, John Maynard. *The General Theory of Employment, Interest and Money*. London: Palgrave Macmillan, 1936.

Klein, Naomi. *The Shock Doctrine: The Rise of Disaster Capitalism*. Toronto: A.A. Knopf, 2007.

Kochan, Thomas A., Adrienne E. Eaton, Robert B. McKersie and Paul S. Adler. *Healing Together: The Labor-Management Partnership at Kaiser Permanente*. Ithaca: Cornell ILR Press, 2009.

Kuhn, David P. *The Hardhat Riot: Nixon, New York City, and the Dawn of the White Working-Class Revolution*. Oxford: Oxford University Press, 2020.

Labor Watch Canada. 15 May 2022. http://labourwatch.com/.

Larrowe, Charles P. "A Meteor on the Industrial Relations Horizon: The Foreman's Association of America." *Labor History*, 2, no. 3 (1961): 259–294.

Lavigne v. Ontario Public Service Employees Union. 2 S.C.R. 211 (1991).

Leacy, F.H. ed., *Historical Statistics of Canada*, second edition. Ottawa: Statistics Canada, 1938.

Levitt, Martin. *Confessions of a Union Buster*. New York: Crown Publishers, 1993.

Loomis, Eric. *A History of America in Ten Strikes*. New York: The New Press, 2018.

Los Angeles Times Archives. "Writers Strike Chronology." *Los Angeles Times*, 4 August 1988. www.latimes.com/archives/la-xpm-1988-08-04-mn-10237-story.html.

Mackaman, Tom. "An Interview with Political Scientist Adolph Reed, Jr. on the New York Times' 1619 Project." *World Socialist Website*, 20 December 2019. www.wsws.org/en/articles/2019/12/20/reed-d20.html.

Mackenzie-King Mackenzie King, William Lyon. *Industry and Humanity: A Study in the Principles Underlying Industrial Reconstruction*. Boston: Houghton-Mifflin, 1918.

Maclean, Nancy. *Democracy in Chains: The Deep History of the Radical Right's Stealth Plan for America*. New York: Penguin, 2017.

Mayer, Gerald. "Union Membership Trends in the United States." Congressional Research Service, Library of Congress, 31 August 2004.

McAlevey, Jane. *No Shortcuts: Organizing for Power in the New Gilded Age*. New York: Oxford University Press, 2016.

McCartin, Joseph A. *Collision Course: Ronald Reagan, the Air Traffic Controllers, and the Strike that Changed America*. New York: Oxford University Press, 2011.

McInnis, Peter. *Harnessing Labour Confrontation: Shaping the Postwar Settlement in Canada, 1943–1950*. Toronto: University of Toronto Press, 2002.

Merritt, Keri Leigh. *Masterless Men: Poor Whites and Slavery in the Antebellum South*. Cambridge: Cambridge University Press, 2017.

Meyer, Gerald. *Vito Marcantonio: Radical Politician, 1902–1954*. Albany: State University of New York Press, 1989.

Meyer, Stephen. *The Five Dollar Day: Labor Management and Social Control in the Ford Motor Company, 1908–1921*. Albany: SUNY Press, 1981.

Miller, Marvin. *A Whole Different Ballgame: The Sport and Business of Baseball.* Secaucus: Carol Publishing Group, 1991.

Millis, Harry A. and Emily Clark Brown. *From the Wagner Act to Taft–Hartley: A Study of National Labor Policy and Labor Relations.* Chicago: University of Chicago Press, 1950.

Milloy, Jeremy. *Blood, Sweat, and Fear: Violence at Work in the North American Auto Industry, 1960–1980.* Vancouver: UBC Press, 2017.

Mills, C. Wright. *The New Men of Power: America's Labor Leaders.* New York: Harcourt, Brace & Co., 1948.

Minchin, Timothy J. *Labor Under Fire: A History of the AFL–CIO Since 1979.* Chapel Hill: University of North Carolina Press, 2017.

National Labor Relations Board v. Kentucky River Community Care, Inc. 532 U.S. 706 (2001).

National Labor Relations Board v. Yeshiva University. 444 U.S. 672 (1980).

National Right to Work Committee, "About the National Right to Work Committee." 30 April 2022. https://nrtwc.org/about-the-national-right-to-work-committee/.

Noble, David. *America by Design: Science, Technology, and the Rise of Corporate Capitalism.* Oxford: Oxford University Press, 1977.

O'Malley, Chris. *Bonds Without Borders: A History of the Eurobond Market.* Chichester: Wiley, 2015.

Orth, John V. "English Combination Acts of the Eighteenth Century." *Law and History Review*, 5, no. 1 (Spring, 1987): 175–211.

Ostroff, Michael, dir. *Many Rivers to Cross.* Ottawa: Canadian Union of Postal Workers, 1999.

Oxford Reference. "Statue of Artificers." 3 May 2022. www.oxfordreference.com/view/10.1093/oi/authority.20110803095426927.

Painters DC30. "Scott Walker Admits to 'Divide and Conquer' Strategy, YouTube." 00:37, 31 May 2012. www.youtube.com/watch?v=EXc5bBTA7wg.

Panitch, Leo and Sam Gindin. *The Making of Global Capitalism: The Political Economy of American Empire.* New York: Verso, 2012.

Panitch, Leo and Donald Swartz. *From Consent to Coercion: The Assault on Trade Union Freedoms,* third edition. Aurora: Garamond, 2003.

Parrot, Jean-Claude. *My Union, My Life: Jean-Claude Parrot and the Canadian Union of Postal Workers.* Halifax: Fernwood, 2005.

Phillips-Fein, Kim. *Invisible Hands: The Businessmen's Crusade Against the New Deal.* New York: W.W. Norton, 2010.

Piketty, Thomas. *Capital in the Twenty-First Century.* Cambridge: Belknap, 2014.

Press, Alex N. "The Class War Is Raging at Amazon's Staten Island Complex." *Jacobin*, 25 April 2022. https://jacobinmag.com/2022/04/amazon-labor-union-staten-island-ldj5-rally/.

Rae, Bob. *From Protest to Power: Personal Reflections on a Life in Politics.* Toronto: Penguin, 1997.

Riding, Jacqueline. *Peterloo: The History of the Manchester Massacre.* London: Head of Zeus, 2018.

Rinehart, James, Christopher Huxley, and David Robertson. *Just Another Car Factory? Lean Production and Its Discontents.* Ithaca: Cornell ILR Press, 1997.

Ritchie, Sarah. "Federal NDP, Unions Happy Liberals Will Include Strikes in Anti-scab Law." *Toronto Star*, 29 March 2022. www.thestar.com/politics/2022/03/29/federal-ndp-unions-happy-liberals-will-include-strikes-in-anti-scab-law.html.

Roberts, Wayne. *Cracking the Canadian Formula: The Making of the Energy and Chemical Workers Union.* Toronto: Between the Lines Books, 1990.

Rosenblum, Jonathan D. *Copper Crucible: How the Arizona Miners' Strike of 1983 Recast Labor–Management Relations in America.* Ithaca: Cornell ILR Press, 1995.

Ross, Stephanie. "Varieties of Social Unionism: Toward a Framework for Comparison." *Just Labour* 11 (Autumn 2007), 16–34.

Ross, Stephanie and Jason Russell. "Caterpillar Hates Unions More than It Loves Profits." *Labour/Le Travail*, 81 (Spring 2018): 53–85.

Royle, Edward. *Chartism*, third edition. London: Routledge, 1996.

Rubio, Philip F. *Undelivered: From the Great Postal Strike of 1970 to the Manufactured Crisis of the U.S. Postal Service.* Chapel Hill: University of North Carolina Press, 2020.

Russell, Jason . *Our Union: UAW/CAW Local 27 from 1950 to 1990.* Edmonton: Athabasca University Press, 2011.

———. *Leading Progress: The Professional Institute of the Public Service of Canada, 1920–2020.* Toronto: Between the Lines, 2020.

———. *Making Managers in Canada, 1945–1995: Companies, Community Colleges, and Universities.* New York: Routledge, 2020.

———. *Canada, A Working History.* Toronto: Dundurn, 2021.

———. "What Will Work Look Like post-COVID-19? It Will Take Us Back to the Future." *Globe and Mail*, 11 April 2021. www.theglobeandmail.com/opinion/article-what-will-work-look-like-post-covid-19-it-will-take-us-back-to-the/.

Russell, Thaddeus. *Out of the Jungle: Jimmy Hoffa and the Remaking of the American Working Class* New York: A.A. Knopf, 2001.

Ryan, Sid. *A Grander Vision: My Life in the Labour Movement.* Toronto: Dundurn, 2019.

Salmond, John A. *The General Textile Strike of 1934, from Maine to Alabama.* Columbia: University of Missouri Press, 2002.

Sanger, David E. with Stephen Greenhouse. "President Invokes Taft–Hartley Act to Open 29 Ports." *New York Times*, 9 October 2002. www.nytimes.com/2002/10/09/us/president-invokes-taft-hartley-act-to-open-29-ports.html.

Savage, Larry and Charles W. Smith. *Unions in Court: Organized Labour and the Charter of Rights and Freedoms.* Vancouver: UBC Press, 2017.

Scheiber, Noam. "Starbucks Union Campaign Pushes on, with at least 16 Stores Now Organized." *New York Times*, 8 April 2022. www.nytimes.com/2022/04/08/business/economy/starbucks-union-new-york-vote.html.

Screen Actors Guild – American Federation of Television and Radio Artists (SAG-AFTRA). "SAG Presidents." 30 April 2022. www.sagaftra.org/about/our-history/sag-presidents.

Sefton-MacDowell, Laurel. *Renegade Lawyer: The Life of J.L. Cohen.* Toronto: Osgoode Society for Canadian Legal History, 2001.

Sexton, Patricia Cayo. *The War on Labor and the Left: Understanding America's Unique Conservatism.* Boulder: Westview Press, 1991.

Slater, Joseph. "Public Workers: Labor and the Boston Police Strike of 1919." *Labor History*, 38 (1996): 7–27.

Smith, Robert Michael. *From Blackjacks to Briefcases: A History of Commercialized Strikebreaking and Unionbusting in the United States.* Athens: Ohio University Press, 2003.

Statistics Canada. "Union Status by Industry," 7 January 2022. www.150.statcan.gc.ca/t1/tbl1/en/tv.action?pid=1410013201.

———. "Union Coverage by Industry, Monthly, Unadjusted for Seasonality." 6 May 2022. www.150.statcan.gc.ca/t1/tbl1/en/tv.action?pid=1410006901

Stefanovich, Olivia. "Supreme Court Sides with Uber Drivers, Opening Door to $400M Class-Action Lawsuit." *Canadian Broadcasting* Corporation, 26 June 2020. www.cbc.ca/news/politics/stefanovich-supreme-court-uber-class-action-decision-1.5626853.

Stepan-Morris, Judith and Maurice Zeitlin, *Left Out: Reds and America's Industrial Unions.* Cambridge: Cambridge University Press, 2002.

Storey, Robert. "The Struggle to Organize Dofasco and Stelco." *Industrial Relations/Relations Industrielles*, 42, no. 2 (1987): 366–383.

Strategic Organizing Center. "Power at Work." 15 May 2022. https://thesoc.org/

Strikwerda, Eric. *The Wages of Relief: Cities and the Unemployed in Prairie Canada, 1929-39.* Edmonton: Athabasca University Press, 2013.

Subramanian, Vanmala. "How Uber Got Almost Everything It Wanted in Ontario's Working for Workers Act." *Globe and Mail*, 25 May 2022. www.theglobeandmail.com/business/article-uber-gets-almost-everything-it-wants-in-doug-fords-working-for-workers/.

Sufrin, Eileen. *The Eaton Drive: The Campaign to Organize Canada's Largest Department Store, 1948 to 1952.* Toronto: Fitzhenry and Whiteside, 1982.

Sugiman, Pamela. *Labour's Dilemma: The Gender Politics of Auto Workers in Canada, 1937–1979.* Toronto: University of Toronto Press, 1994.

Teamsters for a Democratic Union. "Ron Carey: Visionary Teamster Leader Dies at 72," 12 December 2008. www.tdu.org/news_ron-carey-visionary-teamster-leader-dies-72.

The Canadian Press. "Air Canada Back-to-Work Bill Gets Royal Assent" *Canadian Broadcasting Corporation*, 15 March 2012. www.cbc.ca/news/politics/air-canada-back-to-work-bill-gets-royal-assent-1.1268054.

The Economics Daily. "Union Membership Rate 10.5 Percent in 2018, Down from 20.1 Percent in 1983." *US Bureau of Labor Statistics*, 25 January 2019. www.bls.gov/opub/ted/2019/union-membership-rate-10-point-5-percent-in-2018-down-from-20-point-1-percent-in-1983.htm.

The Statutes Project. "1812: 52 George 3 c.16: The Frame-Breaking Act." 4 May 2022. https://statutes.org.uk/site/the-statutes/nineteenth-century/ 1812-52-geo-3-c-16-the-frame-breaking-act/.

Thomas, Mark. *Regulating Flexibility: The Political Economy of Employment Standards.* Montréal and Kingston: McGill-Queen's University Press, 2009.

Trotter, Joe William Jr. *Workers on Arrival: Black Labor in the Making of America.* Oakland: University of California Press, 2019.

United Kingdom National Archives. "Second Statute of Labourers, 1351." 3 May 2022. https://nationalarchives.gov.uk/pathways/citizenship/citizen_subject/docs/statute_labourers.htm.

United Kingdom Parliament. "Trade Union Act, 1871." *International Labor Organization*, 4 May 2022. www.ilo.org/dyn/natlex/docs/ELECTRONIC/ 98373/117044/F1671923749/IRL98373.pdf.

United States Bureau of Labor Statistics. "The Davis-Bacon Act, as Amended." April 2009. www.dol.gov/agencies/whd/laws-and-regulations/laws/dbra.

———. "Union Members – 2021," *Bureau of Labor Statistics*, 20 January 2022. www.bls.gov/news.release/pdf/union2.pdf.

———. "Union Members – 2021." *Bureau of Labor Statistics*, 20 January 2022. www.bls.gov/news.release/pdf/union2.pdf.

———. "Union Members – 2021." US Department of Labor, 20 January 2022. www.bls.gov/news.release/pdf/union2.pdf.

———. "Union Members in Wisconsin — 2021". 16 March 2022. www.bls.gov/ regions/midwest/news-release/UnionMembership_Wisconsin.htm.

———. "Union Membership Historical Table for Indiana." 27 April 2022. www.bls.gov/regions/midwest/data/unionmembershiphistorical_indiana_table.htm.

———. "Union Membership Historical Table for Michigan." 27 April 2022. www.bls.gov/regions/midwest/data/unionmembershiphistorical_michigan_table.htm.

———. "The Triangle Shirtwaist Factory Fire." United States Department of Labor, 4 May 2022. www.osha.gov/aboutosha/40-years/trianglefactoryfire.

———. "Occupational Employment and Wages, May 2021, 29-0000 Healthcare Practitioners and Technical Occupations (Major Group)." 16 May 2022. www.bls.gov/oes/current/oes290000.htm.

Van Elteren, Mel. *Managerial Control of American Workers: Methods and Technology from the 1880s to Today.* Jefferson, NC: McFarland and Company, 2017.

Veldhuis, Niels and Jason Clemens. "To Remain Competitive, Ontario Needs to Follow Indiana and Michigan's Lead." *Fraser Institute*, 15 May 2022. www. fraserinstitute.org/article/remain-competitive-ontario-needs-follow-indiana-and-michigans-lead.

Vinel, Jean-Christian. *The Employee: A Political History.* Philadelphia: University of Pennsylvania Press, 2013.

Volkswagen. "#TBT – The rich history of Volkswagen's Puebla plant." 16 July 2020. https://media.vw.com/en-us/releases/1354.

Von Hayek, Friedrich. *The Road to Serfdom.* Chicago: University of Chicago Press, 1944.

Wayne State University. "UAW – Battle of the Overpass." *Walter P. Reuther Library*, 28 April 2022. https://reuther.wayne.edu/image/tid/1203.

Weir, Robert E. *Beyond Labor's Veil: The Culture of the Knights of Labor.* University Park: Pennsylvania State University Press, 1996.

Weyrich, Matt. "MLB Work Stoppages: History of Lockouts, Strikes in Baseball." *NBC Sports*, 13 March 2022. www.nbcsports.com/washington/nationals/mlb-work-stoppages-history-lockouts-strikes-baseball.

White, Bob. *Hard Bargains: My Life on the Line.* Toronto: McClelland and Stewart, 1987.

Whittaker, Reg and Gary Marcuse, *Cold War Canada: The Making of a National Insecurity State, 1945–1957.* Toronto: University of Toronto Press, 1994.

Wilentz, Sean. *Chants Democratic: New York City and the Rise of the American Working Class.* New York: Oxford University Press, 1984.

Wilt, James. "Remembering the Gainers Strike." *RankandFile.ca*, 6 March 2006. www.rankandfile.ca/remembering-the-gainers-strike/.

Windham, Lane. *Knocking on Labor's Door: Union Organizing in the 1970s and the Roots of a New Economic Divide.* Chapel Hill: University of North Carolina Press, 2017.

Wirenius, John F. "Introduction." In John F. Wirenius, ed., *The Taylor Law at 50: Public Sector Labor Relations in a Shifting Landscape.* Albany: New York State Bar Association, 2019.

Wisconsin Historical Society. "John R. Commons, 1862–1945: The Spiritual Father of Social Security." 20 May 2022. www.wisconsinhistory.org/Records/Article/CS507.

World Trade Organization. "History of the Multi-Lateral Trading System." 5 May 2022. www.wto.org/english/thewto_e/history_e/history_e.htm.

Zinn, Howard. *A People's History of the United States.* New York: Harper-Collins, 1980.

Zuboff, Shoshana. *The Age of Surveillance Capitalism: The Fight for a Human Future at the New Frontier of Power.* New York: PublicAffairs, 2019.

Index

Printed in the United States
by Baker & Taylor Publisher Services